D0711193

Surviving With Kids

A Lifeline for Overwhelmed Parents

Wayne R. Bartz, Ph.D.

and

Richard A. Rasor, Ed.D.

Illustrations by Dick Pike

Impact 🐚 *Publishers*
POST OFFICE BOX 1094
SAN LUIS OBISPO, CALIFORNIA 93406

Copyright © 1978

by Wayne R. Bartz and Richard A. Rasor

All rights reserved under International and Pan-American Copyright Conventions. No part of this book may be reproduced, stored in a retrieval system, or transmitted in any form or by any means, electronic, mechanical, photocopying, recording or otherwise, without express written permission of the authors or publisher, except for brief quotations in critical reviews.

Library of Congress Cataloging in Publication Data

Bartz, Wayne R   1938-
   Surviving with kids.

   Bibliography: p.
   1. Children--Management. 2. Parent and child.
3. Behavior modification. I. Rasor, Richard A.,
joint author. II. Title.
HQ769.B3249   649'.1   78-13328
ISBN 0-915166-55-0

PUBLISHER'S NOTE

This publication is designed to provide accurate and authoritative information in regard to the subject matter covered. It is sold with the understanding that the publisher is not engaged in rendering psychological, medical, or other professional services. If expert assistance or counseling is needed, the services of a competent professional should be sought.

Eighth Printing, March, 1990

Impact *Publishers*

POST OFFICE BOX 1094
SAN LUIS OBISPO, CALIFORNIA 93406

DEDICATION

To our parents, who endured our behavior, and also to Jenell, Brad, Jennifer, Brian, Neil, Tricia, and Shannon, children close to us who challenged our wits and provided some of the examples for this book.

ACKNOWLEDGEMENTS

No book is ever solely the product of its authors. Many people lend their experience and expertise. *Surviving With Kids* is no different. We are indebted to Gerry Patterson for much of this book's research foundation, to Bob Alberti for his careful editing, Alden Paine for his helpful reviews, Mark Ackerman for his insightful evaluation and suggestions, and Carolyn Larsen who typed the manuscript from a frightful rough draft. Our appreciation is also extended to Dick Pike, the creative artist who did all the illustrations. Finally, a word of thanks is given to those closest to us who endured the many time demands and inconveniences of our writing task.

WRB and RAR

Contents

INTRODUCTION

Imagine yourself to be an overwhelmed parent -- you have a couple of very active young children. Their behavior often seems a catalog of pure frustration:

...They make lots of noise that often is ear piercing.

...They make a mess of practically everything they touch.

...They "can't find" toys, shoes, pencils, bikes, socks, pillows or clothes (and neither can you half the time!).

...They often won't eat what's good for them unless you insist upon it. Then they act as if you are trying to poison them.

...They manage to undo a clean house in two minutes. The child's room itself is usually a disaster zone.

...They move at a snail's pace (or disappear entirely) when there is work to be done.

...They are always running when you want them to walk or stand still. If *you* are in a hurry, they are "too tired" to run. You begin to feel older than your years.

...They mysteriously make your favorite things disappear.

...They not only bring out the best in you -- but the worst as well. You fantasize about when they will grow up.

...They delight in pestering you while you're busy. Your anger worries you. Alcohol or tranquilizers don't help!

Happily, at times they also

...run up to you and offer a warm hug when you meet
them at school.

...look across the room while playing and say "I love you,
mommy."

...win a ball game, or bring home an award from a junior
track meet;

...make the honor roll at school;

...pick a bouquet of fresh flowers for May Day;

...collect $25.00 for a charity.

The whole experience of relating to and raising kids can be
at once exhausting and delightful. Yet there are many things
along the way that can be done to reduce the exhaustion and
increase the delight. That's why we wrote this book.

It is designed to be a practical aid to people who want to
improve their relationships with children. It is based upon a
large body of evidence which shows that child behavior can
be changed. The main focus is on pre-teenagers but the
principles are applicable to people of any age. We believe
that children do not have a particularly "good" or "bad"
nature, nor are they instinctively "bratty", "lazy", or
"insecure." Their behavior is overwhelmingly a product of
learning. Although genetic inheritance may set broad limits
upon our capabilities, it is really *learning* that determines
how we behave, within those limits. Children often do not
behave as parents want -- but not *because* they are
"naughty" or "bad". These are labels given as a *result* of
behavior. The way we can change the behavior is for child
and parent to *learn* better ways of dealing with the
immediate living situation.

It has been traditional to explain children's behavior in
just the opposite way. For example, a frequent reason given
for children doing poorly in school is that they simply have a
bad attitude or are poorly motivated. The logical solution

would then be to try to change the "bad attitude." But we don't believe that trying to change an *attitude* is what will lead to most success. Rather, it is being successful in school that will change the attitude! The school must arrange conditions which maximize the opportunity to succeed. Only then will a child begin to like the school experience. Similarly, a parent must arrange home life conditions which will allow for a child to succeed. It is too much to expect any child to suddenly feel confident and positive about anything *before* experiencing success at it. We must stress, of course, that each child is unique and will not necessarily respond in a given situation the same way as another child. Any successful application of psychological principles clearly must be tailored to the individual involved. This book is about relationships. We recognize that relationships are held together by good feelings, and good feelings come from the positive things people do for one another. So this book naturally revolves around ways of doing nice things that make people feel good, and minimizes the need for doing things that make people feel bad. That's what relating is all about!

Hopefully our writing has avoided most of the complicated jargon that psychologists and psychiatrists so often use. (That was hard work for us!) The extensive illustrations help to demonstrate principles, since we believe the notion that "one picture is worth a thousand words." We selected our examples from our own lives and hundreds of situations suggested to us by students and parents. Many of the examples should be familiar and may even bring back memories from your own childhood. Of course, selected examples cannot cover every problem a parent has to face. But with a little imagination the thirty principles demonstrated should be useful over a broad range of life situations. Our examples reflect values held by the parents portrayed in the cartoons. You may have different ideas about what behavior is *desired* in children. Still, the *principles* apply regardless of the behavior involved.

We also believe that people should be parents by choice, with a conscious commitment to the effort involved in responsible parenthood. This means they not only have a *right* to guide the behavior of their children, but a *responsibility* to do so. Active guidance is quite different from the approach which assumes that children need only "unconditional love" to blossom into healthy, happy adults. Constructive guidance and limit setting can be applied with love, and are a realistic preparation for adult life. The world seldom offers permissive, unconditional "love!" The active guidance we advocate is also very different from the heavyhanded approach of "children should be seen and not heard." We encourage parents to be "lovingly firm."

All of us are greatly influenced all our lives -- first primarily by parents, then teachers, friends, television, government, bosses, spouses, and many others who come into the act. Parents *do* influence children, probably more than anybody. They have, as part of their parental responsibility, the right to help their children learn to behave in ways they consider appropriate. At the same time, they have a responsibility to provide a warm and loving relationship that will foster a positive self concept and aid each child to maximize his or her potential. Sometimes these two goals seem to be in conflict, and the decisions are difficult.

We don't pretend that this book gives "all the answers." No book can. What we offer you here is a set of general principles, tested and proved with thousands of parents and children. Used consistently, they will work for *nearly* all parents with *nearly* all children. Nevertheless YOU AND YOUR CHILDREN ARE UNIQUE, and you must decide for yourself how to apply what you learn here.

In order to make such decisions wisely, we suggest you follow a procedure such as the following:

1) Read the entire book carefully;
2) Review principles you are not sure of;
3) Select one or two (no more at first!) areas on which you wish to work with your child;
4) Consider the goals you wish to achieve, the potential outcomes of this approach, and its limitations;
5) If you decide to go ahead, give your choice a chance! It will take some time, and perhaps some *additional* (temporary) problems will occur.
6) Evaluate success or failure in terms of your original goals. Remember that if you try to help your child to learn to express feelings, for example, and then you get upset when the child "talks back" to *you*, that you have been "successful," in terms of your original goal! ("OK, smart psychologist, so *now* what do I do?") The point here is to be careful to establish goals which you -- and hopefully your child -- *really want* to accomplish!

Parents have to make hundreds -- thousands -- of choices and decisions about their children's behavior, and must consider the limits accepted by our society. Being a successful parent of a happy child is a rewarding experience, but also very hard work! We hope this book will make that work a bit easier.

The influence that parents can have on the lives of their children over a period of fifteen to eighteen years is incredible... Whether parents are aware of it or not, through their daily life styles and the consistency of their behavior they teach their children how to blend, for better or worse, the basic ingredients for living -- how to deal with anxiety, failure, how to handle money, make friends, be a friend, how to resolve conflicts and make decisions, how to live and how to be loved...

Research is telling us that healthy, balanced children who value themselves and others are likely to come from homes in which the parents respect and care for the children, each other, and themselves; where there are firm rules which are consistently enforced; and where there are high standards for behavior and performance which children are expected to live up to.

Don E. Hamachek
ENCOUNTERS WITH THE SELF

1. Looking at behavior

"You're aggressive!"

"He's insecure."

"She's intelligent."

"He's paranoid!

How often have you found yourself using such expressions? We all use labels for people in our daily lives, because they help us to classify, sort, and put order into our world, making it easier to understand. One may describe a neighbor as "friendly," a business acquaintance as "ambitious," and a relative or child as an "extravert." This form of labeling helps us get a quick picture of what the person might be like, although we are aware (hopefully!) that it is a limited picture. We don't expect a *positive* label to tell us a great deal about an individual person, since labels are so general (there are many types of people we might call an "extravert"). Ironically, with *undesirable* behavior we sometimes apply a descriptive label and expect that label to *explain* the behavior.

PRINCIPLE 1: Labels - such as "hyperactive," "aggressive," or "insecure" -
really don't explain behavior, nor do they
give parents guidance in how to deal with
their children.

You have undoubtedly seen highly energetic children who
sometimes wear down parents (maybe your own children at
times?). Their attention span may be short, their interests
endless, and they can be "wound-up" day and night.
Thousands of such children have been labeled
"hyperactive" and treated by physicians with drugs, a
practice that is now being seriously questioned. The label
"hyperactive," originally a *name* for certain behavior, came
to be seen as an *explanation* in itself.

Such circular thinking is dangerous. Johnny is full of
energy and runs around a lot. We call that "hyperactive."
Why does he run around a lot? *Because he is hyperactive.*
How do we know he is hyperactive? *Because he runs around
a lot*! Johnny's "diagnostic label" merely *names* what he is
like -- it does not *explain* what causes his behavior.

LABELS, LABELS, LABELS

Do labels really tell us anything about a child? Herman's mother Martha made such excessive use of labels that we could also apply a label to her efforts as well -- "overkill!" While Herman was behaving badly, Martha indulged herself in the luxury of using labels as if they *explained* his behavior. Finally, neighbor Marge used a few choice labels herself!

Look again at what Martha and Marge said. Do the labels *aggressive, hyperactive, artistic, rebellious, brainwashed, nutty head-shrinker,* or *brat* tell you anything useful about what actually happened in this situation? Do the labels really tell *why*? Indeed, you may consider Herman to be a "brat," but his inexcusable behavior is not caused by "brattiness." It is maintained by its consequences, including mother's inaction. Clearly, labels can lead parents into a blind alley. For, if labels *caused* troublesome behavior, then parents couldn't do anything to change their children's actions. Fortunately, this isn't the case!

Some difficult child behavior may have its *basis* "inside the child" -- perhaps a result of body chemistry. Indeed, research is still being conducted to determine if some overactive children could be stimulated by the foods or chemical additives they eat. However, labels have been badly misused. For years we labeled some people as "retarded." Expecting very little from such people, guess what we got? That's correct -- little. Schools, doctors, and parents have overused labels such as *underachiever, culturally deprived, emotionally disturbed, insecure,* and *educationally handicapped.* The result of all of this labeling was often that educators, hospitals, and even parents gave little meaningful help if a child was categorized as "retarded" or "disturbed."

Labels will always be around, but why use them in ways which incorrectly suggest there is little hope for change?

Instead, we suggest you avoid labels and ask instead,
"What is going on here?" "What possible payoffs could
there be for the child to act this way?" "Could I be
accidentally encouraging this kind of behavior because of *my*
actions?"

Starting to look for influences within the environment
rather than within the individual child is a first step in
understanding behavior.

☺

Imagine that Grandma, Grandpa, and a proud new father
are in the maternity ward looking through the window at a
newborn boy. Grandma beams, "He's so cute! He certainly
looks a lot like you, Son." The new father replies, "Yeah, he
does look a lot like me, but he has his mother's hair."
Grandfather says, "Oh, I don't know. I think he has his
mother's forehead, though...One thing is for sure, he's got
the Johnson chin!"

We've all heard such conversations. It's fun to look at a
newborn and try to spot family characteristics. We also try to
be rather "democratic" about it in making sure that at least
one physical characteristic is attributed to each member of
the immediate family. Actually, a day-old baby probably
doesn't show much in the way of resemblance to anybody.
Later on, as physical features become more evident, we may
begin to see some likeness between the young child and
parents or grandparents. If the son develops "frizzy" hair,
and the only person in the family who has hair like that is
Grandpa on Dad's side, we are on fairly safe ground to

assume that the frizzy hair came from Grandpa. Indeed, most of our physical characteristics are inherited.

Many people think of behavior as a collection of personality traits that are also inherited from parents and grandparents, much like eye color or hair texture. The best evidence available suggests that, while the *foundations* for behavior are inherited, most *behavior* is learned through life experiences.

> **PRINCIPLE 2: Behavior is influenced by two major factors: heredity and learning.**

THE "INHERITED" TEMPER

Learning to share toys is a hard lesson, and it's a rare young child who willingly gives up prized possessions to let another use them, even for a few minutes. In the illustration, Mom suggests that Jimmy's temper is a "personality trait" unique to Dad's O'Grady family and Irish origins. But is the temper really something *inside* Jimmy? Actually, anger in such situations is common to children everywhere, and is learned, not inherited. Even very young children see that anger expression sometimes achieves one's goals.

We do not believe that genetics provides an adequate explanation for specific behavior. Children do inherit physical traits and a certain biochemical makeup, which may help or hinder them in various activities. All of these forces, however, interact with what the child *learns* from life experiences.

Inherited physical structure increases the chances for various types of behavior. For example, a child who has inherited a strong and sturdy body is more likely to be involved and successful in sports. A youngster who is attractive is more likely to be outgoing and involved socially. The child who inherits a highly developed brain has the potential to excel in intellectual activities.

The point is, *we don't inherit behavior!* What we do inherit is a broad potential to behave in a million different ways. We don't inherit a bad temper, stubbornness, laziness, or violent aggressiveness. Nor, on the positive side, do we inherit industriousness, friendliness, leadership, courage, or honesty. All of these behaviors and values (often assumed to be characteristics of different social or national groups) are the result of different *learning* experiences, rather than heredity.

For parents, the fact that behavior is determined by learning is actually a great blessing. If all behavior was inherited, we would be stuck with a trait like the "O'Grady

temper,'' never able to change it! No parent can change a
child's genetic structure. Parents can and do have a
tremendous effect upon their children through learning. (We
don't want to leave the impression that parents *exclusively*
determine a child's behavior, however. All sorts of people
get into the act. Also, children certainly influence parents!)
We'll examine this complex-yet-simple learning process in
detail in the rest of the book.

2. Why do children act the way they do?

Have you ever known parents who think their child is an "angel", while you are convinced the child is a "monster?" We do not always agree on what is "good" or "bad" behavior in children. This is also true among nations, cultures, or socio-economic groups. Actions considered "good" in a Northern European country, for instance, may be considered "bad" in the Middle East. And our judgement changes over time: many behaviors considered "bad" for women in the 1920's, such as assertiveness, are considered desirable today. What is acceptable and what is unacceptable is a matter of opinion, but all behavior is *acquired* in the same way, no matter how we *label* it. Within your own family there is probably general agreement about what is acceptable and unacceptable behavior.

Obviously, no one *wants* children to learn "bad" behavior! They often do, nonetheless, and parents can sometimes see where they got such habits, perhaps from neighborhood friends, school, television, or even other family members! Sometimes it seems a mystery: how did the child ever pick *that* up? Why does it continue in the face of punishment? In such cases, parents may be *accidentally teaching* the behavior and helping to maintain it by their reactions to it!

PRINCIPLE 3: Most human behavior is learned. Children learn both desirable and undesirable behavior in the same way.

To illustrate, let's look at examples of children being taught to run to Mom in two entirely different situations.

"HELP, MOM, I'M HURT!"

"HELP, MOM, I DIDN'T GET MY WAY!"

In the first cartoon example, Mom paid attention to a crying child who may have been injured. Upon closer inspection, it was clear that Freddie had not hurt himself seriously, so Mom showed him how to take care of it and sent him on his way. Clearly she was interested in and concerned about his welfare. Most mothers would want a small child to come to them immediately when there is any possibility of physical injury. By her warm response, Mom encourages and teaches Freddie to come to her *when he is hurt*. He learns that Mom gives help and comfort when he needs them.

In the second set of cartoons, Mom paid attention to Billy's crying over a dispute with his older brother. By her warm response, and by directing Timmy to share the wagon, she is encouraging and teaching her son to cry and run to her *when he does not get his own way*. Billy learns that Mom will help him get his way with other children. Most mothers do not want a child to run crying to them over every disagreement or upset. Note that in both cases the behavior is being learned in *exactly the same way*, no matter whether the parent wants it or not.

In the first case, if we asked Mom why Freddie runs crying to her when hurt, she would see nothing surprising about it. "Why, I want him to do that. I fix his little hurts, and make him feel better," she might say.

In the second example, if asked why Billy runs crying to her every time he does not get his own way in a dispute with his brother, this mother might be truly mystified, and say something like, "I don't know. I just can't understand it. I tell him to try to get along with his brother, and I make his brother play with him, but he just keeps on with that crying, always running to me every time they argue."

Mother isn't trying to teach her children to do things that bother her (and which are not in their own best interests), but nevertheless she is doing just that, by paying attention to the very behavior she might not want. Instead, she might have directed the boys to work it out themselves. Other undesired behavior is learned in much the same way: acting defiantly; hurting others; truancy; stealing. The people who do such things have systematically -- even if unintentionally -- been taught to behave in ways society considers undesirable.

Please understand that we do not wish to discourage mothers from comforting their children when they are hurt! On the contrary! The point of this discussion is that touching, hugging, and attention from loved ones are powerful means of strengthening specific behaviors. Thus parents need to be aware of the effect of their responses to their children, and that they are teachers of child behavior -- even if by accident!

The main point we would like for you to remember is that *your child's behavior, whether appropriate or inappropriate, is learned.* The principles involved in that learning are the subject of this book.

Every now and then we encounter parents who are surprised to find out that their child is quiet, cooperative, and perhaps even docile at school. At home, they find the child loud, negative, and almost constantly in trouble. Such parents may see nothing unusual in the observation that their own behavior is very different at home, at work, with friends, or while on vacation. Why not their children as well? We *all* gear our actions to what is expected by the situation.

PRINCIPLE 4: All people, including children, behave differently depending upon where they are and whom they are with.

Children, like adults, learn what behavior fits what situations, so that places, people, and events become "cues" for both desirable and undesirable behavior.

PITY THE POOR SUBSTITUTE TEACHER

Like a green light has been turned on, the class goes wild when the substitute teacher shows up. The students are well aware that Mrs. Praether doesn't know them, can have little effect upon their grades, and probably will not be seen again for the rest of the year. So why work? Why not play or just do nothing, or even enjoy tormenting the substitute? The substitute becomes a "cue" for acting up. When the regular teacher returns, she finds it hard to believe that her normally well-behaved group could possibly have been so unruly.

The immediate effect of cues upon behavior can be seen in a variety of situations. For example, some young children cry when parents are about to go out and leave them with a babysitter. Yet the minute the door closes, the crying stops. Some brothers and sisters will fight noisily when parents are around, yet play cooperatively when alone. Children can also behave ideally at home but cause perpetual problems at school. Situations, people, and places serve as *cues* for all sorts of behavior.

Dick Rasor remembers when, as a child, he rarely would cry when hurt -- that is, until he saw his Mom. Then tears would burst forth. In this instance, the sight of his mother was all the additional cue he needed to put forth a great show of pain -- comforting would soon follow.

Our point is this: children's actions make sense in terms of the situation. Sometimes the cues are very subtle and not noticed. In other cases, they are obvious. When we look at the complexities of each unique individual, and the variety of situations which occur in our lives, it is not difficult to see why behavior can at times seem to be beyond explanation!

3. Everyone likes to feel good

If somebody suggested that your life revolved around a system of reward and punishments, would you agree? As you might have guessed, we would! A reward, as we view it, can actually be almost anything, depending upon individual preferences ranging from hugs, compliments, or self-congratulations on a job well done, to the more material things like candy, gold stars, or money. Whatever it may be, if it represents a good consequence, it will tend to increase the behavior it follows. If you say "Hello!" to someone in the morning and that person nods and smiles back, you will be more likely to say "Hello!" again the next day (assuming you value nods and smiles!). However, if you receive a sneer or snub in response, you will probably stop greeting that person.

> **PRINCIPLE 5: We keep doing things which are followed by good consequences or good feelings (rewards).**

PRINCIPLE 6: We stop doing things which
are followed by bad consequences, bad
feelings, or no rewards.

These principles seem so basic and common-sense that
they may appear hardly worthy of mention. Yet they are of
profound importance, and are misused daily by parents,
schools, government, and business. For example, where is
the incentive for a child to keep doing chores if the effort
goes unnoticed? Why would a student try hard in school if
every attempt earns poor grades and/or parental scorn?
Where is the reward, in a ''planned obsolescence
economy,'' for an automaker to produce a forty-miles-per-
gallon car that will last twenty years?

It is easy to see, and even ''understand'' the basic reward
and punishment principles, but successful application is not
so easy. In fact, most of the thirty principles in this book are
directed toward different aspects of the effective use of
rewards with children.

Consider an example involving conversation between an
adult and a child:

ENCOURAGING CHILDREN TO TALK WITH PARENTS

When Susan said, "Look what I made in school today," her invitation was followed by good consequences: Mom looked pleased and said something positive. When Susan asked if Mommy wanted to know more, she was encouraged to talk about her achievement. By her interest and attention, Mom has actually "rewarded" showing and talking about the project. Because of Mom's warm actions, we can expect that Susan will continue to talk to her mother about school and probably about other things as well.

In our next example, another Mom does something different:

DISCOURAGING CHILDREN FROM TALKING WITH PARENTS

This mother also gave her daughter attention and a smile for showing what she made in school, but here the similarity ends. In this case, Mom really *discouraged* any talk about the child's achievement, and Carol can assume that her Mom wasn't interested and wanted her to go to her room. In effect, Carol was *punished* for trying to tell Mom about her achievement. If this were to happen very often, we can predict with some certainty that the child will seldom try to start conversations with her mother in the future.

We have all seen children who are outgoing, talkative, and who seem to enjoy conversing with adults. In contrast, we also have seen children whom we might call "shy" or even "withdrawn" -- children who don't say much and who will answer a question with very few words, or may not even answer at all. It appears that some children have been taught to be outgoing and others to be shy through a system -- intentional or unintentional -- of rewards, or lack of them.

We are not saying that parents must always instantly stop whatever they are doing and pay attention to a child who has interrupted! That is a good way to teach the child to interrupt! However, parents who wish to intentionally encourage behavior they like must make an attempt to reward it, and that may mean making an extra effort. In our example, it may mean listening to explanations and "kid-talk" that is frankly not too interesting to an adult.

Nevertheless, the long term benefits to the child -- particularly in the area of human relationships -- will also be benefits to the parents.

Another common example: children often learn not to talk with their parents about sex. Youngsters are not encouraged to express their curiosity, or may even be actively discouraged and socially punished, forcing them to get their sex information elsewhere. While most everyone agrees that sex education should come from parents, few parents

actually teach their children to ask questions about sex in a
direct, honest manner.

We have given simple examples here of reward and
punishment. More complex examples will follow in later
chapters. The reward principle is the foundation of most of
what is known about human behavior. It applies to all
behavior, all people, and all ages. It is as true when dealing
with yourself as it is with others. *If you want a behavior to
continue, reward it.* If it is not rewarded in some way, at
least some times, it will not continue.

Nearly every living creature is attracted to situations that
bring on good feelings and is put off by painful events. We
humans, the most complex of living things, are strongly
influenced by our various emotions. Depending upon our
personal experiences, particular people or places *become
associated* with good or bad feelings. Such feelings may
persist years later.

Try now to recreate some of your own childhood
experiences and feelings. Sit back, close your eyes, get
relaxed, and breathe deeply. Think of a very close person
from your childhood such as your father, mother, or a friend.
Imagine you are with this person, reliving an experience
from your childhood. Spend three or four minutes with your
imagination and notice any changes in bodily feelings. Go
ahead and do it now...

...If you really were able to create a vivid memory, you may
have experienced strong feelings or emotions, some positive
and maybe some negative. If childhood experiences are
predominantly pleasant, a child will grow to adulthood
having good feelings associated with those experiences --

with Mom, Dad, school, and friends. But, if a child is routinely treated badly within the family or by other adults, he or she may grow up feeling uncomfortable and perhaps even hostile or resentful around those persons (or even adults in general). It is not surprising that such children react against parental figures. At any time of life we can acquire such feelings.

> **PRINCIPLE 7: Our learning experiences determine when we feel such natural emotions as love, elation, anxiety, and sadness.**

If a very young boy is spanked or otherwise hurt several times while in the presence of a nice, fuzzy white rabbit, we find that he begins to show signs of alarm at the mere sight of the rabbit. On the other hand, if he gets hugs and smiles while he's with the rabbit, he will begin to feel good when he sees the animal. Such feelings can last months, years, or even a lifetime, unless he has an experience which modifies this learning.

This process of learning by association is known more formally as "classical conditioning." It tells us simply that objects or events which are grouped together in time, place, or situation often enough tend to be associated, and therefore call up the same feelings. We develop fear or fondness for anything as a result of what it has been "paired" with in our early learning experiences. Seeing blood, for example, may lead to crying, if the sight of blood is repeatedly associated with pain. Given enough such pairings of blood with pain, the sight of blood alone can generate fear and crying, even when physical pain is absent. Similarly, if good feelings, smiles, and loving are regularly associated with a particular person, just the thought of that person will likely result in a "warm glow." Here are a couple of examples:

LEARNING TO FEEL GOOD ABOUT SOMEONE

Uncle Stan is obviously a special person in Joe's life. When Uncle Stan came for visits, he helped Joey feel good by doing fun things with him that were appropriate for his age. So, later memories of Stan and his name produce good feelings.

A lifetime includes hundreds of people (teachers, aunts, uncles, parents, friends, brothers or sisters) who can bring about memories and emotions, pleasant or unpleasant. Ideally, in a family, Mom and Dad want to create situations, events, and relationships with children that produce good feelings for both parents and children. People who experience good feelings in their day-to-day lives also tend to have good feelings about themselves. The best way to teach children to value themselves and to be good parents someday, is to make their childhood happy.

LEARNING TO FEEL BADLY ABOUT SOMEONE

Even the most well-intended efforts of adults don't automatically result in good feelings for children. Uncle Harold meant well, but he was rough and inflicted pain upon Billy every time he saw him. When continued over the years, Harold himself became a "pain" and even his name produced bad feelings twenty years later.

It is easy to attach emotions to names. If you were trying to pick a name right now for a newborn son, which among the following would you be *least* likely to pick? And why?

Adolf
Throckmorton
Richard
Dagwood
Charles
Huckleberry

Since all names are originally neutral, upon what basis do we make a choice? It is because names take on meaning and produce feelings through association, some positive and some not so positive (perhaps some even sound ridiculous). There is nothing strange about how we come to feel good or badly about people, places, or events.

4. Each child is unique

When we were children, many households had a ready supply of graham crackers, "Kool Aid," or fruit punch, which were often used as rewards (for doing chores, keeping "out from under foot," small successes at school or on the ball field, ...). At that time, there was not the variety of "children's goodies" on the market which there is today. With the tremendous range of crackers, cookies, candies, and drinks available now, a parent cannot assume that a graham cracker will have the value for children that it did when we were young.

Obvious? Perhaps, but we have seen parents become astonished when a child rejected a "reward" that was offered. The *parent* considered the item as a reward; the child's reaction demonstrated clearly that it was not!

PRINCIPLE 8: Because each person is unique, rewards must also be unique -- that is, "tailor-made" to fit the individual.

A PENNY ISN'T WHAT IT USED TO BE

When Grandpa was a child, getting a penny from his parents or grandparents was a big thing and he remembers it vividly, so he assumes that his grandchildren will consider it a great reward.

It is simply an economic fact that today's penny is not worth much. When Grandpa was a youngster, it might have purchased a respectable amount of candy. To these children his suggestion of a "big surprise" evidently meant something else. Often bedtime is also a time of conflict since children don't like to get ready for bed and leave adult company. It is a rare young child who *admits* to being tired and wanting to go to bed! In this case the big surprise turned out to be no real surprise at all, leaving the children upset and perhaps feeling cheated, and Grandpa hurt and perplexed. His gesture of love was not seen by the children as generous, despite his caring intent.

This type of outcome happens in different ways at different ages. Parents sometimes offer "dinner out" as a reward, having in mind a really nice restaurant. But where do the *kids* want to go? A pizza parlor or fast food place! Besides avoiding the assumption that children will like what parents like (or did like when *they* were children), we need to keep in mind the likes of individual children.

The illustration on the following page is another example of the importance of individualizing rewards.

TEEN-AGE INDIVIDUALITY

Going camping for the weekend may be a "thriller" for Dad, and may have been for the kids when they were younger. But now dating and activities with friends have become very important. They may be more valued than spending the weekend with the folks. So this "reward" is actually only a reward for one of the children, and may even be a punishment for the son who would miss the dance. Dad comes up with another reward, a traditionally "masculine" outing like fishing, which Dad assumes will appeal to his son, while Mom does the same thing with her daughter, assuming that shopping and hair setting will appeal to her because she is female. Fortunately, in recent years such sex stereotypes have come seriously into question, so that now boys and girls can feel free to do many things which might have been denied them in the past because they were "unmasculine" or "unfeminine." So if the parents in our illustration are tuned into their children's *individual* needs and desires, the son will get his hair-styling and the daughter her fishing trip. (Hopefully, Mom and Dad will also get some special time with the children!).

If parents are to be effective in the use of rewards, they need to do a lot of questioning, observing, and testing to find out who likes what. We just can't make assumptions about what others like. There is no universal reward for all people of all ages.

As parents, we can't assume that children necessarily like what we like, that what one child likes will be liked by another, that children's preferences will not change over time, or that the sex of the child will tell you what he or she might like. The entire notion is summed up nicely in a recent popular slogan: "Different strokes for different folks."

When we talk about rewards and their use with children, a common reaction from parents is, "Why, you're talking about a system of bribes!" This concern is expressed so often that we want to give it special attention.

Advocating the use of rewards with children is nothing new -- it is the *systematic, planned* use of rewards that is important. All of us spend our lives in a constantly changing system of rewards -- from early parental hugs and affection to gold stars in school, and on to letter grades and diplomas. As adults we have paychecks, promotions, status, as well as interpersonal rewards from relationships with family and friends. It seems when people express a concern about "bribes" it is not *rewards* they are objecting to, but the specific use of money as a reward, or objects purchased with money. Note, however, that hardly anyone considers a paycheck from work to be a bribe, nor do parents think of a weekly allowance for their children as a bribe. And it is ridiculous to think of a hug, or a smile, or other spontaneous expression of love as a bribe!

So "bribe" is really a loaded word. To most people the word suggests some kind of shady deal, a payoff for something that shouldn't really be done. "Reward" and "bribe," then, are not the same thing. A reward is a tangible expression of approval. A bribe is a payoff for something illegal or of questionable ethics.

With parents, this problem seems to come up most in situations where they assume the child "should" do something because of "duty" or self-motivation. In such situations parents often see any sort of reward as being unnecessary or excessive, especially if the child doesn't want to do something a parent thinks he or she should want to do. They may even feel that what the child really needs is a good "kick in the rear." Yet we must remember that all of us do things because of the rewards involved -- some immediate, some distant, some from ourselves, some from others. Children are no different. It may take different rewards to motivate them.

"Well," we have heard parents protest, "once you start rewarding children they won't want to do anything without a reward. Are you going to follow them around the rest of their lives giving out rewards?" Of course not. We do not suddenly "start" rewarding children. Their world is already full of rewards (and punishments). Parents can become *systematic*, however, using those rewards that are preferred by individual children to motivate them toward desired behavior.

A child who is not learning to read may dislike reading because of the experience of failure. The parent may think the child should "want" to read. If nothing is done, the result is a non-reading child, who falls further behind. Instead, the parent or teacher can use some kind of simple reward, such as points, tokens, or gold stars, to get the child *started* reading and to motivate practice. As the child experiences success, that reward will no longer be necessary because reading itself, and the expanded horizons it offers, become rewarding. Nobody has to follow a reading child around for the rest of his or her life rewarding reading! But you may indeed have to offer extra incentive to the non-reader for those first attempts, in order to get that youngster started.

All parents are rewarded in a variety of ways for the things they do. Some of the ways are obvious (such as money or fame), and some are much harder to see but no less effective (self-congratulations or the respect of valued friends). These are not bribes for us, nor are our children's prized rewards bribes for them! Systematic rewards merely bring the natural learning process under a degree of control.

What kinds of material rewards do you value? The list might include a nice home, clothes, jewelry, cars, perfume, boats...just about anything money will buy! Of course children have their prized rewards too: candy, cookies, dolls, toy trucks. *Material* rewards (as we use the term) are tangible objects that have some economic value.

There is another very important class of rewards -- the

social variety. Social rewards are intangible, cost nothing, and there is no limit to supply. Some of the most important ones for children are attention, praise, smiles, affection, touching, and laughter. When it comes to social rewards, it is interesting to note that adults respond to the same things that children like. In fact, most of our adult interactions and relationships are based upon social rewards.

There are also a few rewards that seem to fit into both categories, material objects that have primarily social value, such as gold stars, points, or grades. For adults, rank, position, titles, and maybe even medals, qualify.

PRINCIPLE 9: We all like material rewards such as money, food, or toys. But it is really social rewards like attention, praise, and affection that make us feel good about ourselves.

Social rewards are far more important than material rewards in changing behavior. Granted, most of us would like to have lots of material possessions! Wealth can indeed make life easier, but happiness and feelings of satisfaction with life depend upon a great deal more than just material wealth. Social interactions -- human relationships -- give life its warmth and vitality. No one ever gets tired of good friendship, love, appreciation, concern, or interest from others!

Never underestimate the power of social rewards! Long term change doesn't come about from candy, cookies, or gold stars. Meaningful behavior change comes from relating to children with love and care.

Let's look at two situations involving report cards and social rewards:

REACTION TO A REPORT CARD

ANOTHER REACTION TO A REPORT CARD

In the first set of cartoons, Ken's Dad rather mechanically gave out a material reward. He showed little interest and no real enthusiasm except for the cash. Certainly Ken will enjoy the money, but the human social reward, so important between father and son, seemed to be missing.

In the second cartoon example we find a constrast: Dad responded with interest, showed pleasure in his facial expression, in touching his son, and in telling Rob how proud he was. He also gave out a material reward, but the situation is rich in social rewards. Rob will feel gratified, proud, and happy with this experience...certainly a great improvement over the first businesslike transaction.

The use or non-use of money for grades is not really the issue here. Some parents feel OK about giving a "bonus" for good grades, while others do not. The point is that, whether or not money is used, *the real reward in terms of the parent-child relationship is the social reward. That is the one that will have the greatest long-term effects.* We should note that the use of a material bonus for children's grades is in no way different from what happens with many adults who get something special for a "job well done." Any kind of bonus is in part a social reward, too, since it calls attention to the person's behavior and singles it out for recognition. But, like the child example, a bonus paid to Dad by his boss personally, with a pat on the back and a comment about how good a job he does, will certainly have more effect than just a check that shows up in a pay envelope without comment.

One final observation concerning the parent who fails to use social rewards: We sometimes hear young people say, "My dad was OK, I guess, but he never gave anything of *himself.* Oh, he would give me money and buy me junk, but there was no feeling between us." Or from father, "After all I did for that kid he still doesn't seem to respect me. I don't understand it. I bought him everything he wanted." Obviously material rewards are not enough!

☺

5. Parents do have influence!

Not long ago a worried mother said to us, "I don't know why David is always right at my feet. It seems he just won't leave me alone for an instant. I try to get him to play by himself with interesting toys. I've told him to go into his room or play with other children. I've even spanked him, but nothing seems to work. I don't know...this whole thing is probably due to the divorce, and now he's insecure." Indeed, a divorce may cause adjustment problems for people working out a new lifestyle, but chances are David pesters his mother because she accidentally rewards him, even though she wants him to stop. Her looks, touches, scolds, and even spanks are still attention to David. To help him through the divorce adjustment, Mother needs to give him plenty of reassurance and attention -- but to carefully avoid doing so at times when David is acting in unwanted ways.

> **PRINCIPLE 10: Attention is one of the most powerful social rewards, for both desirable and undesirable behavior. Even scolding a child is paying attention, and may be rewarding!**

Although it may seem obvious that attention can be a social reward, we want to emphasize not so much the obvious forms of attention (yelling out, touching, grabbing), but the more subtle forms, such as a glance, smile, frown, eye contact, or physical gesture. In many families there are troublesome child behaviors that are maintained by exactly these types of subtle attention rewards.

ATTENTION MAINTAINING AN UNDESIRABLE BEHAVIOR

If we were to question Susan's mother as to just what was going on in the illustration, she might tell us that she first tried explaining the situation to Susan, then asked her to go outside (repeated by Dad), and then suggested something else to capture Susan's interest. Indeed, those things happened. But what else was Mom doing? She was giving repeated attention to the very behavior she wanted Susan to stop, thereby actually offering subtle encouragement to continue interrupting, asking questions, and staying in the room! Even Dad, by looking at Susan during these exchanges -- however "harshly" -- gave an attention reward.

What else could these parents have done? How about simply ignoring the undesired behavior? "What," you say, "How could they just ignore it?" We're going to save a detailed answer to your question for Chapter 7. For now, the point is that the parents in this example are actively involved in *teaching* Susan a behavior through social rewards, despite the fact that it is the exact behavior they did not want! To change the situation, they will have to markedly change their use of attention. It is a simple application of the principles of reward and attention: If children are getting the love and attention they need, and if they learn that they will not get them by remaining "underfoot," or by tantrums, or by interrupting adult conversations, such problems will diminish (in time, and with considerable patience!).

Many parents and teachers alike operate under the mistaken belief that publicly noticing "bad behavior" will somehow stop it (indeed, much of our society operates on this erroneous premise). "Johnnie, Mother is watching." "Don't go in there!" "Leave your brother alone!" "Put that down this instant!" Imagine a teacher looking out at her class: "Who is talking over there? Is that you, Peggy? Stop it right now! I expect to have absolute quiet in here." Often kids giggle when a teacher reacts like that. Or the teacher may say: "Cindy, get back in your seat. What are you doing on that side of the classroom?" Is the teacher's public notice going to stop the behavior, or is it actually an *attention reward* for the child? Aren't the talkers and walkers in that classroom being actively rewarded by attention? Many studies have demonstrated that such attention produces more and more of the very behavior teachers want to end in their classrooms.

It is important to note, of course, that teachers and parents do not have control over *all* of the rewards (attention, in this example) which the child may receive in the situation. Disruptive classroom behavior, for instance, is powerfully rewarded by the attention of other children. In such cases, it may be necessary to use other procedures to eliminate the behavior.

We have heard a number of amusing examples in which college students purposely used attention in the classroom to markedly change their professor's behavior without his/her knowledge of what was going on. One professor we knew tended to give very dull lectures, reading in a monotone from his notes. Yet on rare (and most welcomed) occasions he would digress from the notes and describe interesting personal experiences related to the topic. Three students sitting in the front of the classroom agreed privately to look bored and inattentive during lectures from notes, but to look very attentive and smile immediately when the professor talked about personal experiences. Within two weeks the professor, who did not know about the "experiment," was not referring to his notes at all. Such is the power of attention and other social rewards!

"Monkey see, monkey do" was a popular saying among parents when we were kids. The slogan didn't have much to do with monkeys but rather reflected a common observation of parents that children learn a great deal by just watching the behavior of others. Author James Baldwin sums it up: "Children have never been very good at listening to their elders, but they have never failed to imitate them."

> **PRINCIPLE 11: Much of our behavior is learned by imitating the people around us, particularly parents.**

This principle probably is no great surprise to anyone, yet parents sometimes forget that very alert eyes and ears are frequently tuned to them. Through the modeling process a child learns values, attitudes, gestures, vocabulary...and bad habits. Consider the simple ritual of eating. If a child spends an average of an hour a day eating with parents, that child has a daily opportunity to imitate them in the ways they eat, types of food eaten, tone of conversation, speed, food sequence. If you calculate the total number of those eating hours during the child's first 12 years, you will find that it amounts to 4,380 hours! Imagine how much a child must learn from parents after that many hours of observation! It's a bit staggering when we consider the number of hours children actually spend observing and imitating the full range of adult behavior.

Young adults often deny that they are like their parents. Certainly specific behaviors might be quite different. Yet psychologists have found that the best *single* indicator of what a person will be like as an adult is what the parents were like. For instance, grown children are likely to belong to the same political party as their parents, and to have similar religious beliefs. (Yes, we can think of exceptions, too!)

During the growing years, children are exposed to a tremendous variety of "models" they can imitate, including their parents. Playmates (particularly older and well-liked ones), school teachers, and heroes/heroines on TV, all serve as role models. It is really interesting to compare estimates of the total number of hours available (through age 12) to be influenced by those four categories of models:

APPROXIMATE NUMBER OF HOURS
SPENT IN PRESENCE OF MODELING INFLUENCE
(0-12 YEARS)

PARENTS
19,000 HOURS

TEACHERS
5,000 HOURS

TV
13,000 HOURS

OTHER CHILDREN
14,000 HOURS

Parents are clearly the most powerful childhood models, because they are such a dominant part of the young child's world. But the older children get, the stronger other influences become.

A comment about TV: Research studies have shown that children readily imitate models who have high status and prestige and who are seen to be rewarded for what they do. Television personalities, superstars, and fantasy characters certainly have status, are often idolized by children, and almost always are rewarded for what they demonstrate on the screen.

There has been much debate and concern about TV violence and its effects upon kids. We don't claim that watching a murder scene will necessarily cause an increase in the homicide rate. It's not that simple. Yet the question must be raised: Just what *are* we teaching children with TV? Our time estimate allowed the average child three hours per day watching TV, but we have seen estimates for American children as high as seven hours per day!

Nobody wants children to imitate TV violence, yet according to one government study (U.S. National Commission on the Causes and Prevention of Violence), during an average TV viewing week the programs contained over 600 acts of violence. More than half the major characters (the models) inflicted violence on someone else. Violence occurred in 95% of the televised cartoons. Such violence is often given from "good guys" to "bad guys" so it fits within our concepts of good versus evil. Can anyone realistically maintain that 12 years of exposure to this will have no adverse effect upon children? We doubt it. At the very least it desensitizes us to the pain and suffering of others. And at the worst...?

6. "Too much love" never hurt anybody

"The children now love luxury. They have bad manners, contempt for authority, they show disrespect to their elders...They no longer rise when elders enter the room. They contradict their parents, chatter before company, gobble up danties at the table, cross their legs, and are tyrants over their teachers."

Does any of that sound familiar? It is attributed to the Greek Philosopher Socrates some 2,000 years ago! No doubt parents of every generation have had a commentary on the spoiling of youth. OK, let's take a look at this concern in some detail.

A "spoiled child" usually gets his or her own way regardless of parental wishes. Sometimes they can be annoying or even downright obnoxious. Still, some parents tolerate it and wonder why the troublesome behavior continues. Such parents usually avoid any contradiction of the child's wishes and often give the impression that they want to be very popular with their chidren. Because they give many material and social rewards to children, it is only natural to wonder if it isn't the *rewards* that have spoiled the child. The fact of the matter is that the child has been *taught* to behave in an obnoxious manner, not intentionally, but by giving rewards *for the wrong behavior.*

> **PRINCIPLE 12: Parents need not worry about giving "too much" love and affection. The way to "spoil" a child is to reward undesirable behavior.**

We want to emphasize, it is not an overabundance of rewards that results in a child behaving badly, but the non-systematic use of rewards. If a child is rewarded for all actions, we can expect to see a continuation of both good and bad behavior.

The end result of years of this inefficient training is that the child's behavior gets worse until parents are so frustrated they don't know what to do. Some seek professional help. They feel love for their child, yet are "driven crazy" by the child's behavior. Such parents may be so constantly angry that they can scarcely contain their hostility, perhaps saying, "I don't understand it, we've done everything for the boy, we've been good providers, we've loved him, and yet he's always in trouble. At times I could wring his neck!"

The key to understanding lies in looking at *how* a child is being rewarded.

WHEN THE CHILD SAYS ''NO'' - SOCIALLY REWARDING DEFIANCE

Mom, by being nice and consoling, is hoping Cindy will change her mind and cooperate. Her idea may be that if she gives love when there is defiant behavior there will no longer be a need to be defiant. She explains, and finally gives in, changing her shopping plans (and inconveniencing her friend) to fit Cindy's whim. While we might admire Mom's patience and her attempts to help her daughter understand the situation, she is nonetheless socially rewarding defiance with attention, touch, verbal warmth, concern in her voice, and giving in. If this sort of interaction continues, we can predict that Cindy's rate of saying "No" will be maintained and may even increase. Mom is demonstrating how to start "spoiling" a child.

WHEN THE CHILD SAYS "NO" - ANOTHER APPROACH

This Mom, like most mothers, knows that kids will be defiant now and then, and will test the limits of parental patience. But instead of stopping everything and socially rewarding defiance as in the first example, this Mom pays minimal attention to it and doesn't let her daughter's "no" interfere with plans. In effect, Mom is teaching Sally that saying "No" doesn't win -- there is no reward for acting defiantly. If Mom is consistent, Sally will try this tactic less and less.   Ideally, Mom might have planned not to take her child shopping in the first place as children sometimes find such errands boring and tiresome. But, if the situation (such as the one shown here) demands that a child comply with a reasonable request, Mom must "stick to her guns" and insist upon compliance with a minimum of fanfare. Resistance to unwelcome tasks can often be avoided if a small treat for everybody is promised ahead of time, such as an ice cream cone or a few minutes of play at the park. (Caution: Don't make such an offer *following* an act of defiance!)

We are not suggesting here that children should ideally be like robots who unquestioningly jump and obey every parental command. Children have rights too, including expression of their own desires and sometimes not wanting to participate in errands or do chores. In this example, Mom acknowledged her daughter's legitimate feelings about not wanting to go, but asserted the parental right to make the decision.

"Spare the rod and spoil the child," was a popular child-rearing maxim for our parents' generation. Often it was interpreted as simply meaning that children should be punished frequently, as if punishment in itself were somehow good for them. We don't believe that, and will discuss punishment in a later chapter. However, "spare the rod" can also be interpreted as suggesting parents should set limits and guidelines for children -- not letting them do everything they want. We will agree with such an interpretation wholeheartedly. It has been our experience that children really want parents to set guidelines and define limits of behavior.

Rewarding "bad" behavior, by repeatedly giving in or being permissive, teaches a child to behave badly. Do this for several months -- maybe even years -- and you have a spoiled child...and later, perhaps a spoiled adult. So, parents should feel free to give lots of love and other social rewards. *The key is that such social rewards are not given to any and all behaviors, but selectively to the behavior we like and want to increase in our children.*

None of us would like to be called a "miser." It suggests someone stingy or selfish. But misers are not just the Ebeneezer Scrooges who hoard money. Any of us can qualify as a "social reward miser." The necessary characteristics are: (1) Rarely show genuine interest in others; (2) Do not laugh with others; (3) Be cynical about what others are doing; (4) Fail to compliment others on their deeds or achievements; (5) Keep a safe distance from others.

Think of people in your immediate life situation, such as relatives, friends, employers, acquaintances. How many of them in your judgment would qualify as social reward misers? Finally, how good are *you* at giving out social rewards?

Some parents are social reward misers with their children and don't even recognize it. Often they feel that children "should" do things out of a sense of duty for the family unit.

> **PRINCIPLE 13: Children will not continue. to do things (such as chores) just because parents say "you ought" or "I told you to;" there must also be some good consequence (reward).**

"Children should obey their parents, children should keep themselves and their room clean, children should get good grades, children should do their chores..." All of these are familiar "shoulds" for children. Society has similar ones for adults: Adults should pay their taxes, adults should work hard and be productive, adults should obey the speed limit. Yet, many people do not follow these adult "shoulds" solely out of a sense of responsibility. How many citizens would pay their taxes on time if the IRS didn't care? Would all of us go to work and be productive without a paycheck? Would everyone obey speed limits without a highway patrol?

Similarly, with children, many "shoulds" don't mean much unless there is some kind of reward (or perhaps even punishment) system involved to back them up. Unfortunately, "shoulds" often imply the threat of punishment if a chore is not completed. Usually parents or children whose lives revolve around "shoulds" are carrying a load of fear or guilt. Parents who are social reward misers frequently expect children to do things out of *shouldisms* backed by a threat of punishment.

Some parents learn to be social reward misers because they were treated that way as children themselves. Our most intensive training in being parents, as discussed in the last chapter, comes from our own experience of childhood.

If children are misbehaving and parents are becoming increasingly irritated, there may be less and less social rewarding -- good training for becoming a reward miser! It is very difficult to give social rewards to someone who makes us angry. This is a vicious circle because, as we stop using social rewards, the other person, whether child or adult, has less reason to behave in desirable ways -- so things get worse. When we ignore people who are doing things we want, we make it likely they will not do those things in the future.

It's far better to acknowledge that children, like adults, need social rewards to keep doing the things they must do. Eventually a child will mature to a point where self-given rewards (self-congratulations) will become predominant. Still, we all like a pat on the back for doing tasks which are not terribly pleasant.

Skimpy use of social rewards will likely result in children not wanting to behave as the parents would like, and may increase the use of threats, punishment, and finally bad feelings within the family.

SCROOGE OF THE SOCIAL REWARDS

Dad uses himself as a noble example but fails to give any real social rewards to his son. If Donald continues to do his chores, it won't be because of Dad!

Adults often get caught in "miser traps." While growing up, for instance, men get the message that they are supposed to be strong, silent, and somewhat emotionless. This often leads to being skimpy with social rewards. We hear a common complaint from unhappy wives: "My husband rarely says anything nice to me. He doesn't tell me he loves me. He hardly touches me unless he wants sex. I get no appreciation for all the work I do." The husband who believes that his "manhood" is reflected best in a strong, silent, and non-affectionate approach will very likely turn off both wife and kids.

Another trap affects divorced parents. Mothers often have custody of children while fathers have visitation rights on weekends. Sometimes such a situation allows Dad to make Mom *appear* to be a material and social-reward miser. When the kids spend a weekend with him they get to do everything they like and have all his attention. Then when they go back home to Mom, who has the day-to-day living responsibilities and cannot provide "instand Disneyland" all the time, they see her as "no fun" and a miser. Such a situation can deepen the wedge between the divorced parents and certainly doesn't help the children either. (In such a case, it's desirable that the divorced mother express her concern to the children, talk over the situation with her ex-husband, and try to work out a compromise.)

We earlier outlined some of the dangers of being a social reward miser and also emphasized that parents who use lots of social rewards with their children for the right behavior will be more effective as parents. Just having children behave in ways that we like is a tremendous reward for us as parents! In addition to that, parents who give an abundance of social rewards will receive the same from their children.

The whole idea of popularity, of being liked by others, is based upon this fundamental rule: *you get what you give.*

PRINCIPLE 14: People who give many social rewards to others tend to receive the same in return.

Just as parents socially reward children, children socially reward us as parents, by doing what is asked of them, having a generally cheerful disposition, smiling and laughing, acting excited and happy when they see us, showing affection, and imitating our behavior -- in short, by making us feel needed and loved.

CHILDREN SOCIALLY REWARDING DAD

Dad uses social rewards with the kids, and he gets rewards when he comes home. The children showed obvious pleasure by verbal and physical affection, excitement, and by attempting to get him into their play activities. Dad can't help feeling good about his kids and his arrival at home.

As children grow into the teen years there is often a marked change in their world of social rewards. They have many friends at school, an entire social structure outside the family, and often come to value those outside sources of social rewards more than those at home. Parents often wonder what happened. They feel that their children no longer consider them so important. There may be truth in this, but if parents give a lot of social rewards (even to teenagers), it is reasonable to expect that teenagers will reciprocate. Teenagers can socially reward parents by showing affection (although perhaps toned-down), having a sense of humor, talking and consulting about their lives, showing interest in what parents do, and not treating them as if they were horribly old-fashioned.

Finally, this principle applies not only between parents and children but is true with any two individuals: brother and sister, husband and wife, employer and employee, or friends. If you want to receive social rewards, you need to give them!

7. With a minimum of fear and discomfort

What can you do with a child who disobeys, or throws temper tantrums, whines, cries or screams? One possibility is to pay no attention to it at all! This applies to any undesirable behavior which can actually be ignored without harm to the child, other people, or property.

PRINCIPLE 15: One way to eliminate an undesirable behavior is to consistently and permanently ignore it -- never reward it, even with attention.

There are a few situations and behaviors that *cannot* be ignored. These include:

Children physically hurting or endangering themselves. We cannot ignore a child putting a screwdriver into an electrical wall socket or wandering onto a busy street.

Children physically hurting or endangering others. We're not talking about "routine" fights between children but rather about situations where one child could seriously inflict injury upon another, such as with a rock, hammer, a big stick, or even a fist. This also includes children physically assaulting parents. No one should be expected to ignore an angry child kicking one's shins!

Children damaging or endangering valuable property. We have to intervene if a child is breaking things like furniture, drawing on the walls, or ruining somebody's clothes.

Undesirable behavior that is being rewarded by others, not by parents.

The above-mentioned behavior exceptions clearly require more of parents than just ignoring. But keep in mind that great numbers of the day-to-day child-behavior problems faced by most families *are* maintained simply by parental social rewards and can be changed or eliminated by use of the ignoring principle. We advocate using ignoring whenever possible because it avoids unpleasantness (unlike the use of punishment) and requires only a simple removal of social rewards. When correctly done, there is no payoff *of any kind* for the child's behavior from the parent. Behavior not followed by any kind of a reward will eventually drop out.

THE INCURABLE THIRST

Mom constantly rewards Jackie with her attention, calling back and forth, and ultimately giving in. Jackie has been *taught* to continually ask for a drink of water because Mom will eventually bring some. And even if she doesn't, Mom is fun to talk to from the bedroom! Mom may wonder why this goes on night after night. Why do *you* think it continues? What *could* Mom do?

THE CURABLE THIRST - A DIFFERENT APPROACH

Before going to bed, Mom made sure Ted had a small drink of water. This eliminated the possibility that he was really thirsty. The first time there was a call from the bedroom, Mom responded, *making it clear she will not continue to answer.* This let Ted know that Mom was indeed present. From that point on she ignored all requests, *never* making the mistake of giving in.

If you are going to use this approach, it is important to explain to the child exactly what you are going to do, and then to follow through without fail. This may mean that you will have to ignore an irritating behavior time after time, and maybe even hundreds of times, before it starts to disappear. In fact, it often happens that troublesome behavior which is suddenly ignored increases for a while before it begins to taper off. Success requires time and absolute consistency. The easiest mistake to make is to ignore, ignore, and ignore, and then finally give in. This can only teach the child to try harder and be more persistent next time.

A common parent reaction is that it is very difficult to ignore obnoxious behavior, and parents feel they shouldn't have to endure it. "Do you mean that when John throws a temper tantrum, kicking and screaming on the floor, I'm supposed to look the other way? I can't ignore that! I'd give him a good whack!" Our answer is, "Yes, just ignore it." Why? First, this is a behavior that *can* be ignored even if there are guests in your house. Admittedly, it is not going to be pleasant. But if it is ignored without further reward, the behavior will drop out in time, without the use of physical punishment. Punishment involves a variety of bad feelings which should be avoided whenever possible. Also, punishment may deliver a "mixed" message, because it includes attention, a social reward. So "a good whack" might help to eliminate the tantrums, but it might not. More on punishment later in this chapter.

Extensive research on temper tantrums has shown that ignoring is the most reliable and effective approach for eliminating such behavior. Tantrums are nearly always maintained *purely* by adult attention, whether that be spanking, yelling, grabbing, or giving in to whatever the child wants. Ignored, it will eventaully drop out. So, take a deep breath, and give it a try!

When parents use the ignoring principle with children, it is important to note that something additional is also happening -- the child is suddenly being put on a *reduced* "diet" of social rewards. Since parental attention and social rewards are so essential to children's happiness, *the parent should be sure there is no actual reduction in the total number of social rewards. This can be done by increasing rewards for desired behaviors.* If the child has been getting a lot of attention for throwing tantrums, any improved behavior following ignoring should be richly rewarded. The net result is that the child's undesirable behavior drops out, good behavior increases, and the overall quantity of adult social rewards is at least equal and may even increase. If the child were to lose many social rewards as tantrums cease but no other social rewards appear for other behavior, the child may try to regain that attention and parental concern through another obnoxious behavior. *So don't stop rewarding, just stop rewarding the behavior you don't want!*

When a child doesn't obey, do you ever feel like playing the role of top sergeant and yelling something like, "You get in there and clean your room or you'll get a spanking!!!"?

It's no secret to any parent that strong warnings can work. That is, young children may instantly comply to avoid a spanking or whatever. We can see many situations including "avoidance learning" in our daily lives. For example, we take aspirin for a headache, not because we like its flavor but to give relief from the pain. In fact, most medicine is designed to either prevent or get rid of discomfort. The billions of pills people consume annually are testimony to the power of this principle:

PRINCIPLE 16: It is rewarding to experience a sense of relief when we avoid or escape something unpleasant.

Parents often use nagging, criticizing, scolding, or warnings to get children to behave. Children wish to avoid these discomforts and will behave -- usually just often enough to escape the unpleasantness and thereby reward the parent for nagging, criticizing, scolding, or warning! Thus, parents and children accidentally teach each other to behave in ways neither likes!

USING WARNINGS TO GET A ROOM CLEANED

Obviously Dad is upset at the cluttered room but expresses his anger toward the child personally. He makes a vague threat of punishment and Susie obeys largely out of fear. The whole situation brings about negative feelings for everybody. Dad would now probably find it difficult to compliment his daughter no matter how good a job she does cleaning up her room. And Susie, still upset, would find it hard to accept a compliment from Dad anyway. Granted, the room is being cleaned, but the entire exchange between father and daughter has been colored with bad feelings.

Let's look at another example:

GETTING A ROOM CLEANED - A DIFFERENT APPROACH

In this case Dad may be upset over the room, but instead of directing his anger at Sharon and creating negative feelings, he focuses his attention on the room, and insists that it be cleaned before she plays any more. The entire situation reflects the fact that "the room looks bad" rather than "the child is bad." As the room is cleaned up, Dad is able to compliment Sharon, and the child can feel good about the compliment. Though this episode is not exactly one of happiness, neither is it loaded with anger or fear.

It should be pointed out that this example assumes that Sharon and Dad agree on what a "clean room" really is! Dad may have to be specific in giving directions to her: ''Please put your clothes in the dresser.''

USING WARNINGS TO GET A CHILD INTO BED

It is obvious that this ''countdown,'' similar to the launching of a missile, produced sudden acceleration, but only at the last second when the end of the count had been reached. Many parents, like Jacqueline's mother in the example, use the countdown technique, and no doubt it works. But it becomes a chance to test just how far a parent will go, sort of a fun game for any child! The game may be ok with the parent, but it doesn't take long for children to figure out how to use the countdown as a way of making parents "perform." The problem is that children are actually being taught to stall, fool around, and delay, which can anger the parent. Nevertheless, it is the parent who has taught the child to delay. Some parents are not consistent in using the countdown. One time they use it, another time they do not. Or a parent may count to ten on one occasion, yet only reach five on another. This can be confusing to a child.

GETTING A CHILD INTO BED - THE IDEAL SITUATION

In this case, Mom told Lisa that bedtime was approaching, then rewarded her verbally and with a kiss for getting into bed. That should help her to get to bed on time in the future. But what happens if she doesn't go?

GETTING A CHILD INTO BED - A DIFFERENT APPROACH

Mom has reached the point where going to bed is not something to be stalled, debated, or negotiated. She had already told Dorothy to be in bed, the girl disobeyed, and now she must take the consequences: Mom tells her to get to bed immediately and speeds her along with a *mild* smack on the behind. Dorothy learns that Mom means what she says.

We do *not* advocate that parents use warnings or threats to get children to obey. Nevertheless, in the real world there are times when parents have to have obedience from their children and may need to give an ultimatum. *If you use an ultimatum, back it up. Make it clear what is expected, how soon, and what will happen if the child does not comply. Make the consequence immediate. Never give an ultimatum you cannot or will not carry out!*

Consider this situation: We were at a Southern California beach one beautiful day and observed an interesting interaction between a mother and her 5-year-old son. The boy was in the water playing and Mother said, "Come on, now, it's time to go." The child looked up, then went back to playing. Mother, obviously annoyed, yelled louder. "Johnny, come here right now." He ignored her. She yelled again, even louder. "If you don't come here this instant, we're going to leave without you!" She stood there watching him continue to play. "We're leaving," she called, then began walking toward the car while looking back at him. He looked at her, smiled, and continued his play. Finally, very angry, she splashed out into the water, grabbed his hand, and dragged him toward the car. What did she do wrong? Consider her ultimatum. Everyone, including the child, knew she was not really going to leave him behind and was therefore making an empty threat. When the child tested her on her ultimatum, he learned that it was a bluff.

What is most important about using ultimatums is that parents must mean what they say. Then children will eventually realize that what parents say will be carried out. Of course, as children grow older, their parents issue fewer ultimatums. Adults do not give each other ultimatums if they want to get along together!

One of the notable aspects of the principle of avoidance is that *children* can train their *parents* by using it! It happens often. Let's say that a young boy knows how to do something that really irritates or annoys a parent, such as whining, crying, yelling, or pestering. He wants to buy candy, so he finds Dad and starts whining. He whines, whines, and whines some more. Finally, Dad gets angry. What happens next is crucial. Dad can ignore him, physically punish him, send him to his room, or...you guessed it!...give him the money. "Will you just get out of here and quit bugging me!" Dad says while handing him some change. The boy leaves and Dad sighs to himself, "That kid is going to drive me nuts." He may be right! Look carefully at what just happened: The child whined and whined, and what was the result? He was given money for candy. His whining was rewarded; it paid off! Dad escaped from something unpleasant (he got rid of the whining) so he was rewarded too. *Both* have been rewarded, one by getting something nice, the other by getting rid of something unpleasant.

We can predict that the child will continue to whine (and perhaps become a master at it), while Dad might give in to his whines even faster. They are caught in a vicious circle, and it was all accidental.

Many people successfully get others to do things by bugging them. Kids do it with tantrums, tears, whines, hits, destructive acts, pouts, "I hate you," and a thousand other antics. Adults do it to each other by nagging, ignoring, withholding love or sex, insulting, threatening violence, and in other ways.

Remember, try to keep threats to a minimum. If you feel

you must give an ultimatum, make the consequences clear and back it up. Finally, be sure the communication is clear. Stop to think about what you are saying!

A MISSED MESSAGE

Punishment influences behavior, and fast! That's why it has been around as long as humanity and will probably continue to be around in the future. Punishment is defined as applying an unpleasant consequence (either social or physical) following a behavior. But it's a bit like nuclear power: while having great strength, it also has its dangers. For example, punishment used alone does not teach a new correct behavior, nor does it build positive feelings between people. You cannot separate pain, either physical or social, from the person who administers it. And since punishment does not teach what behavior is desired, it is critical that a parent show or demonstrate what *is* the appropriate way to behave. It is not enough to assume that children can figure out the right way of doing things when being punished for misbehavior. *Show them, tell them, guide them toward the right way.*

PRINCIPLE 17: Punishment is a way of stopping behavior that simply cannot be ignored. If punishment is to be used, it must be clearly related to the behavior, given immediately, of low to moderate intensity, and certain to occur.

PUNISHMENT - AN EXAGGERATED EXAMPLE

Admittedly, this is a tongue-in-cheek example, but the principle still applies. Mother side-stepped her responsibility for administering punishment on the spot and saved it for Dad later. He is then greeted at the door with unpleasant family business (to him this is like being punished for coming home). Dinnertime, which should be a family's pleasant and relaxing time together, becomes a situation loaded with unpleasant feelings. Dad called Johnny a "bad boy," a very negative label and not very specific.

What he meant was that Mom and Dad didn't like what he did. Consider the difference between ''I don't like *what you did*, it makes me mad,'' and ''I don't like *you*, you make me mad.''

USING PUNISHMENT - A DIFFERENT APPROACH

In this illustration, punishment was immediate but calm. It was also related to what Jimmy had done, and the amount of punishment seems about right. We believe that parents should inform each other when they have disciplined a child. In this case Dad supported Mom's decision, which is essential, especially because he wasn't even there when the event happened. Nor was Dad confronted with bad news when he walked in the door. As a result, dinnertime can be free for pleasant kinds of family interaction.

PUNISHMENT - AN INEFFECTIVE APPROACH

Aunt Martha's home, since she does not usually have youngsters around, has not been "Kid-proofed." It has fascinating and breakable things sitting around within easy reach. Ideally, she would have a few toys for visiting children to play with, but since she doesn't, it is Mom's prime responsibility to keep Stevie from getting into things -- perhaps by bringing toys with her. Mom's verbal commands have no effect, the only consequence being that eventually she has the child sit with her. From Stevie's point of view, disobeying Mom resulted in personal attention and getting to sit on Mom's lap, which is a treat. Mom, Aunt Martha, and even Stevie feel more comfortable with Stevie contained in Mom's lap. However, what Mom has unintentionally done is to reward Stevie for misbehaving!

Many parents, when feeling uncomfortable about what their child is doing, will try to stop the behavior by holding or cuddling the child. It does stop the behavior for the moment, but in the long run it teaches the child that misbehavior can lead to loving and cuddling. The misbehavior probably will continue in other situations similar to visiting Aunt Martha's.

PUNISHMENT - A DIFFERENT APPROACH

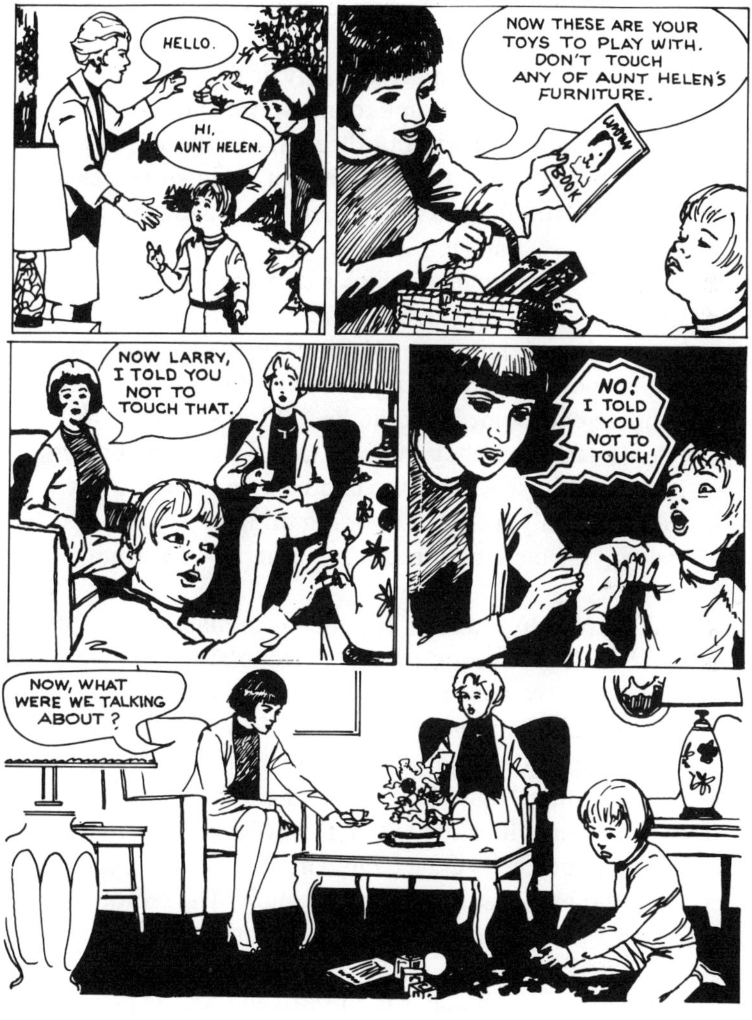

Mother identified the undesirable behavior and intervened quickly. She did not reward Larry in any way other than the minimal attention necessary for the appropriate punishment. Nor did she allow the episode to upset talking with her aunt.

"Time Out" is an alternative to physical punishment which allows a parent at home to intervene and stop unacceptable behavior without threats, hitting, or pain. It means "time out from rewards," either social or material. It is a little like "standing in the corner," but with some added features. To use Time Out:

Select a boring place. Pick a room or closed-off place within a room that can be made free of anything interesting or dangerous to the child. This might be a utility room (with all dangerous articles removed) or another bedroom. It should be lighted and not scary (Don't use a closet or shower stall). It must be boring to the child. Never use the child's own bedroom since that is usually full of interesting things. "Go to your room," for most children, is no real time out from rewards.

Keep the time short. The idea is to place the child in Time Out, thus stopping the unacceptable behavior, and then to release the child after about five minutes of quiet and calm. The child should be told, "That's bad behavior. Go to Time Out." If he or she refuses, quietly and firmly take the child there. Once in Time Out, the child is told that after five minutes of *quiet*, Time Out will be over. The five minutes starts from the beginning of calm and quiet. The child learns through this process that quiet will be rewarded.

Do not talk. The door is closed and there is no verbal interchange between parent and child. If the door is opened, that means another minute in Time Out. The parent decides when the time is up.

Do not debate. Don't spank, don't argue, don't get into a dialog. Time Out must stand by itself.

The Time Out approach has been found to be very effective in dealing with troublesome behavior. It avoids the problems associated with physical punishment and also keeps rewards to a minimum. *It should be used with caution, neither scaring nor hurting the child in the process.* Once again, "loving firmness" is the rule.

We cannot encourage parents in the use of threats, intimidation, fear, physical or social punishment to get children to behave. There are entirely too many undesirable side-effects and there are also better alternatives, as illustrated in our other principles. Punishment has its place -- in *temporarily* stopping a behavior that simply cannot be tolerated or ignored. It also gives parents a chance to immediately teach a more appropriate behavior once the disruptive behavior has stopped. But punishment, if used excessively, can only hurt both parent and child, and sour the relationship. It should be kept in mind only as a less desirable method of behavior change. The methods in order of preference are:

1. Reward the behavior you like.
2. Ignore behavior you do not like.
3. Give verbal warnings that will be backed up.
4. Put the child in Time Out.
5. Punish.

It should be clear by now that the most desirable behavior-change approaches are the first two, because only those avoid significant bad feelings between parents and children.

Why is punishment so popular among parents if it is actually the least desirable method of behavior change? The answer is that the person doing the punishing *gets rewarded* by the abrupt halt in the disliked behavior. Remember, when we do things that help us escape or avoid unpleasantness, we will tend to do them again. In short, the punisher is rewarded by punishing. And punishment is easy. It takes no planning. Unfortunately, some parents become very punishment-oriented.

8. Catch 'em being good!

Listen to a young mother's complaint: "But there's nothing I can reward, he's always naughty!" Consider her statement carefully. Is there really a child who does *nothing* deserving of a social reward? Is any child *always* naughty? No. There is behavior that this mother can reward, but she just isn't aware of it, or perhaps chooses to ignore it. To be fair to her child and to herself, she must switch to a positive focus, starting to actively look for and attend to good behavior.

A classroom experiment demonstrates our next principle impressively: A student is selected and asked to leave the room. The class then picks a simple action for that person to carry out in the room, such as pulling down the motion picture screen or picking up an eraser. The volunteer is called back into the room and told that he or she is to do something simple and not embarrassing, and that the way to find out what to do is to move around the room and listen to feedback from the instructor. In one situation the volunteer gets feedback in the form of a verbal "Wrong!" spoken for every move or action in the incorrect direction. In the other situation the volunteer is given a verbal "Right!" every time a move or action in the correct direction is made. We can then compare the effects of focusing upon the wrong or right behavior. The difference is striking. The student being told "Wrong" wanders around, confused, stopping, starting, and stopping again, rarely reaching the goal except after considerable time. Even if the goal is reached, students who experience this role report feeling upset, stupid, and really

put down. In contrast, students given positive feedback
move consistently toward the goal, usually get there rapidly,
and feel good about the performance. Which approach
sounds better?

**PRINCIPLE 18: It is preferable that
parents have a "positive focus," actively
looking for good behavior in their children
and rewarding it.**

Examples of desired behavior which may be rewarded,
depending upon the age level of the child, might include
going to bed, getting up, playing quietly (or noisily, if you
prefer!), eating a meal, saying "thank you," talking with
adults, doing schoolwork (even partially), learning a new
game/word/skill, reading a magazine/newspaper/book,
getting dressed for school, carrying groceries, putting toys
away, NOT interrupting an adult conversation, NOT spilling
food, NOT teasing sister/brother...The possibilities really
are endless!

Compare the following two examples:

A NEGATIVE FOCUS ON HOMEWORK

If you were a parent whose child brought home a paper with half right and half wrong, which would you focus on? Admittedly, 50% by most standards is not a very high score, and you would want your child to do much better. The key question, then, is what approach will be most successful in motivating better performance? In the first example, Mom is not encouraging as she focuses upon how many answers Carolyn missed. She not only punished the bad work, but ignored the good work as well. In fact, she also punished showing-homework-to-Mom. Carolyn can easily discover that one way out of the homework problem is to not bring papers home!

A POSITIVE FOCUS ON HOMEWORK

In the second example, Sean's Mother had a positive focus. She rewarded getting five right and gave Sean encouragement toward doing even better. She recognizes his success, limited as it was, and sets an expectation of better things to come.

A positive focus is desirable at all stages or places in life, from infancy through old age, at home, on the job, with friends, or in a marriage. Recall the basic reward principle: If a behavior is to be repeated, it must be followed by good consequences. In order to give a reward, one must notice the desired behavior. Without a positive focus, we cannot efficiently use the reward principle. It's surprising that many parents fail to use positive focusing even in obvious situations. How many parents make a point of rewarding small children who are playing quietly and cooperatively? Indeed, they are more likely ignored until some sort of disturbance is heard! How many parents of teenagers make a point of complimenting them when they do chores correctly, talk on the phone for only ten minutes, study properly, or come home for dinner on time? It's too typical for parents to ignore these desirable actions, then to get on the kids when they misbehave in some way. How many adults ignore their spouse's good cooking or nice appearance, yet make a point of griping when dissatisfied? The popular term is "taking things for granted." We call it "failure to focus on the positive."

Upon first exposure to this idea there is often a "gut reaction" against it. The response may be, "Why should I have to reward somebody for doing something they *should* be doing anyway?" "Why should I reward my child for work that is not up to standard?" Well, then, consider the alternatives and their effects. If we ignore behavior we like, it may drop out. If we punish performance that does not match up to our standards, we are also punishing whatever effort went into it. Even if it is hard at times to use a positive focus, and one may have to work hard at doing it, the effects are predictable, positive, and ultimately to the benefit of everyone concerned.

Failure to use a positive focus with others, does something to oneself. One may become the kind of person who always looks for the bad in people and ignores the good, a prime target for such labels as "sourpuss," and "grouch." Nobody wants to be around somebody who is always griping, nitpicking, and cutting away at others. Remember, we get what we give. A grouch will notice that the world is filled with other grouches!

A brief review

Let's take a look at what we have discussed up to this point:

Most human behavior is learned, not "born in," and is the result of influences from the world around us. We tend to do those things which are rewarded and to stop doing those things which are ignored or punished. We will have good and bad feelings connected with people and events, depending upon whether they are associated with good or bad feelings in the past. Parents have a great influence on children because of the importance of social rewards, and even a glance from Mom or Dad can be a strong social reward. It is important to keep in mind that children are individuals too, and rewards must be personalized. There is no danger of spoiling anybody by giving him or her too many social rewards -- unless they are given for undesirable behavior. We all like to feel good, and if we give out lots of social rewards to others, we will get them back in return. Nobody loves a miser! Sometimes children do things we don't like, and while the *easiest* way to deal with it may be by punishing, we suggest that you: first ignore it while rewarding some other desired behavior; then give a clear verbal warning; then try "Time Out;" and *only* if those don't work should you resort to punishment.

All of this leads to a consistent way of relating to people, a "positive focus." *Look for the things you like and reward them* -- that's the best way to guarantee they will continue in the future!

9. Self-esteem is worth working for

Recent comment from a frustrated mother: "My daughter is always getting into things, doesn't mind, and is really getting on my nerves." We have all heard comments like this from parents, which tell us only that the parent is concerned about the child's behavior. There is not enough information included to know specifically what the child is doing, nor to suggest any possible remedy.

> **PRINCIPLE 19: To change behavior, it is first necessary to "pinpoint" -- that is, identify the behavior in question so that it can be both observed and counted.**

This frustrated mom said the child is "getting into things." What does that mean? *What* does the child actually *do*? *When, where,* and *how often*? Mom might reply, "Well, she gets into cupboards and drawers without asking." Better. Now, *which* cupboards and drawers and what does she do when she gets into them? "Just yesterday she took the clothes out of my bureau drawer and piled them on the floor." Good! *Now*, we have pinpointed the behavior so that we can work with it. We cannot deal with "getting into things," because it's too vague. But we

can *observe* and *count* how often a child opens a drawer
and empties the contents. Only by knowing how often the
behavior occurs can your effectiveness in changing it be
determined.

The beleaguered mother also told us that her daughter
"doesn't mind." What does the girl *do* that leads to this
conclusion? Mother answers, "When I ask her to do
something she just doesn't do it." We still need an
example of what might be requested, and of the daughter's
response. Mom says, "One example I can think of is, I
asked her politely to clean up her room. She said she
would, but didn't do it." We must then determine if this
was also true for other requests, such as "helping with the
dishes" or "going to bed." Mother then becomes even
more specific about the "problem area" requests. We can
then determine *specifically* which requests are routinely
ignored. Only at that point have we pinpointed the behavior
"doesn't mind," and can begin actively working to change
it.

Some examples of pinpointed behaviors that can be
observed and counted: hanging up clothes in the closet;
being dressed and ready for school at 7:30; saying "No";
using cuss words (specified); finished eating (all or
specified amounts); minutes of piano practice; crying;
interrupting conversations; taking out trash; hitting another
person; saying "thank you." Once parents have specifically
pinpointed behavior, *then* they can begin to bring about
change.

It is simple to test yourself on the use of this principle.
Think of a child behavior that you like and want to increase,
or one which you find annoying. Put down in writing what
you would call it and how to identify it. Now, ask yourself
three questions: Can I see it? Can I count it? Could another
person using my description also see and count it exactly as

I would? If the answer to any of these questions is "no," the behavior has not been pinpointed.

We'll discuss counting and record keeping more in Chapter 12.

Remember the times when you were amazed by some of the tricks performed by animals on TV or at an amusement park? A porpoise jumps through a hoop, a killer whale gives somebody a piggyback ride, or Lassie plays hurt. These performances were taught by trainers who are very familiar with one of the most basic of learning principles, one which applies to animals and humans alike.

> **PRINCIPLE 20: Learning a new behavior is a step-by-step process. Generally, the smaller the steps, the easier the learning.**

To apply this principle:
1. Divide into small consecutive steps the pinpointed behavior you want to teach.
2. Teach each step, through description, imitation (modeling) where necessary, and liberal rewards for success at each step.
3. Once a step has been mastered, have the learner practice it with all the other steps leading up to it, continually reviewing the entire sequence from the beginning.

4. Proceed in this step-by-step process until the entire
   behavior sequence has been mastered. Large success
   follows many small successes!
Consider this ineffective approach:

*TEACHING A YOUNG CHILD TO MAKE HIS BED
- AN INEFFECTIVE APPROACH*

Mother asked Kent to start making his own bed without
first demonstrating exactly what the steps are. She
mistakenly assumed he knew how to do it because he had
seen her do it. Kent does what he thinks is an OK job and
waits for Mom. But she says (by her words, posture,
expression, and tone of voice) that he didn't quite come up
to par. She gave no encouragement for the work he did and
she fell into the trap of doing it herself (Unfortunately,
Kent learns that Mom will probably do his work for him if
he does it poorly!). She also failed to arrange for a small

enough step that he could successfully accomplish. Kent still has not learned any of the steps involved, nor has he experienced any real success in what he did.

USING THE STEP-BY-STEP APPROACH
IN TEACHING A CHILD TO MAKE HIS BED

Mom asked Kim to do only a small and easy segment of a total learning task. She demonstrated how it was done and asked him to imitate her behavior. She also rewarded him with her touch, a big smile, and praise. Finally, she let Kim know what he will learn tomorrow. It may be that she will have to repeat the first steps a number of times before he is fully successful. At this point Kim has worked at the first steps in bed-making and probably experienced a feeling of success in the process.

Let's look at another situation:

GETTING A CHILD TO DO HOMEWORK
- AN INEFFECTIVE APPROACH

Kevin apparently has no set study time. After dinner he is allowed to get interested in a TV show and then is told to go do homework. This makes homework even more unpleasant than it would be normally, and puts Mother in the position of being like a warden. Kevin stays in his room for half an hour, which is a substantial effort if he actually spent it on homework, but is treated by Mother as if nothing had been accomplished. Instead of rewarding the half-hour of work and allowing a "break" from study, she actually punishes the child's efforts by sending him back to the bedroom.

Unfortunately, the entire interaction has been primarily unpleasant. Homework for Kevin probably is a genuine pain. He has been taught merely to stay in his bedroom, not necessarily to study, and studying has been associated with missing television. To cap it all off, because other family members get to have fun while he doesn't, the entire homework-TV situation can only seem unfair to him.

GETTING A CHILD TO DO HOMEWORK
- A DIFFERENT APPROACH

Here, there is a clear time to study. Mother socially rewards Brent with praise and touch after a short interval of study. She also monitors his work (to be sure he is actually on the task), arranges for a short break after a half-hour of work, and at the end of the evening rewards studying with praise and choice of a TV show. This situation has a pleasant tone, even though "studying" itself may be unpleasant for Brent.

A footnote concerning study habits: children usually enjoy watching TV. Parents can arrange study schedules so that weekly programs become rewards for study time. In this way studying does not mean missing favorite shows, but serves to earn time to watch those shows. Such scheduling may vary from day to day, but should be planned ahead of time. Things that children enjoy can be used as rewards for other behaviors they need to do but do not particularly enjoy. The example of Brent involved television, but it can apply to telephone privileges, radios, phonographs, camping trips -- whatever.

We find that for practical reasons the bedroom is usually the place used by children for study. This presents a problem: kids mainly sleep and play in bedrooms. Therefore, most of the "cues" in the bedroom suggest something other than doing homework, hardly helping to maintain a mood for studying! Many of our college students tell us that they get sleepy while stretched out on their beds studying. Big surprise! Ideally, for effective study there should be a separate, comfortable place, well lighted and free from distractions, where only studying occurs. We recognize that such ideal conditions are not always possible. The main idea is that the study area itself should serve as a *cue* for studying, just as a kitchen serves as a cue for eating! Helping your child to find or create a "study-only" area will be a major step toward improving school work!

10. Kids can't wait

A father says to his 12-year-old son, "Tom, how would you like to earn a trip to Disneyland next summer?"

"Hey, that would be great, Dad!" the boy replies enthusiastically, "What would I have to do?"

"Just get that room of yours cleaned up, and keep it that way!"

"OK! It's a deal!"

Two weeks pass, and the father notices that Tom's room is just as big a mess as it ever was. What happened?

Most of us, given the choice, prefer our rewards immediately following our actions, rather than having to wait until a later time. This is especially true for young children, who do not understand the concept of time and delayed rewards as adults do. Children think in the "here-and-now" -- not in terms of hours, days, or weeks later. To a young child awaiting a promised reward, the end of the day or the end of the week may seem "light years" away. (Remember, a few hours is a much greater percentage of a child's total life than of yours!)

> **PRINCIPLE 21: Ideal timing for rewarding a child is immediately following the desired behavior. The longer the delay between behavior and reward, the less the effect upon learning.**

As we get older, we are more willing to tolerate delays between our behavior and rewards, such as a monthly paycheck. The importance of immediate rewards is really not lessened, however, for we still expect some kinds of continuing social reward at work, such as attention, recognition, or verbal praise. The size of the monthly paycheck is not the most important factor in job satisfaction for most people. Instead, things like a friendly working atmosphere, feelings of self-worth and accomplishment are far more important. Among the beauties of social rewards are that they can be given immediately and there is no end to the supply.

With any age it is important to socially reward right away. Hug, smile, compliment! If material rewards are also to be given, it is not always possible to give them immediately. However, one can give some sort of immediate symbolic or "token" reward such as gold stars, points, or "happy faces" drawn on paper. These tokens in effect provide "credit" that can later be cashed in for material rewards, and thus bridge the time gap between behavior and consequence.

GIVING A DELAYED MATERIAL REWARD
- AN INEFFECTIVE APPROACH

Mother wants to improve Amy's dressing in the morning, so she decides to use both *social* and *material* rewards. The night before, she tells her daughter what the material reward will be. Amy does get ready on time, is socially rewarded, but then discovers that the material reward will not be given until later. That afternoon may be a very long time away for a 4-year-old and, by the time Amy gets it, the material reward may seem unrelated to getting dressed on time.

GIVING A DELAYED MATERIAL REWARD - A DIFFERENT APPROACH

Margie's Mom did not want to give toys during the rushed period just before school. Instead, she rewarded Margie both *socially*, with verbal praise, touch, and smile, and *materially*, with the gold star. The child may enjoy touching, seeing, and pasting up the star herself. Later it will be redeemed for a toy. Such tokens are like money or small gift certificates: they don't have any real value alone, but can be cashed in for something desirable. It is essential, of course, that Mom carry out her promise and cash in the star *that afternoon*.

GIVING THE "BIG REWARD" - AN INEFFECTIVE APPROACH

Dad decided to use a highly prized material reward to motivate his daughter to do even better in school. Indeed, Sonya may do better in school and earn the new bike. However, there are some potential problems here. He has not pinpointed just what higher grades mean, nor what Sonya must do in order to bring up her grades. There is no effort to keep track and to reward steps leading to better grades. Also, the one big material reward is a long time away. There is nothing wrong with giving a bicycle for better grades if that is acceptable to both parents. It is, however, a bit like working six months for one big paycheck!

GIVING THE "BIG REWARD"
- A DIFFERENT APPROACH

Instead of just promising a bike for better grades, Dad pinpointed the behavior that will count as improvement, and proposed a plan to work toward that goal, step-by-step. It involves monitoring Julie's behavior and using points as tokens to give her tangible evidence of progress toward her new bike. Of course, they will have to work out the details of such a point system. Julie will be directly responsible for her own progress, and will have immediate and consistent recognition for her efforts. In addition, the parents are dealing directly with the *behavior* involved in grade improvement -- that is, studying and daily performance. Material reward systems based solely upon grades at the end of a term often fail because they do not reward day-to-day efforts.

These examples involve large material rewards (eg. a bicycle) for desired behavior. We want to reemphasize that handing out such rewards alone -- particularly if done in a cold manner -- will not accomplish what is desired. It is essential that immediate *social* rewards be given for the efforts of children (and adults!). Remember, praise, smiles, touch, and hugs are what *really* count in helping people of all ages to feel loved, respected, and appreciated.

Finally, while it is important to reward *others* immediately, that holds true for *one's own* efforts as well. Often accomplishments will go unnoticed by others, not because they don't care, but because they are busy, preoccupied, or just fail to notice. We have all experienced waiting for somebody to compliment some nice thing we have done, but the compliment never comes. It is easy then to say to oneself, "Why bother?" Such silent suffering is self-defeating.

When you do something nice that goes unnoticed, you can "prompt" another person (whether adult or child) into noticing it. It's perfectly OK to help people notice the nice things you have done. If you prepared a special dessert and your children didn't respond or act differently, what could you do? Ask them how they like it! When parents fail to notice something children have done, the youngsters too may come and tell Mom and Dad about it.

We need all the social rewards we can get, so when we earn them let's make sure to be on the receiving end! It's unrealistic to expect that somebody else will always give us those important rewards without prompting. Children can be taught to prompt and to compliment others as well.

Now, at last, you are ready to *change* a child's behavior. You have pinpointed the behavior in question, used a positive focus, broken it down into small steps, and have selected rewards that can be administered immediately. It is now essential to be highly alert so the child can be rewarded every time the desired behavior (or step toward that behavior) occurs. You want the child to "get the message" about the behavior as quickly as possible. The way to do this is to give the message loudly, clearly, and often. That may mean using a liberal amount of social rewards, token rewards, and even material rewards -- anything that clearly communicates your satisfaction and pleasure to the child, and which the child finds rewarding.

PRINCIPLE 22: There are two basic schedules of rewarding: every time and occasionally. It is best to start by rewarding the desired behavior every time it occurs. Eventually a parent can change to an occasional schedule.

Once the new behavior is happening regularly (over a number of days), a parent can begin to gradually "thin out" the system of rewards. Certainly you don't expect to follow a child around for weeks or months rewarding a behavior every time it happens, nor is that needed. For example, if a small boy is being taught to say "Thank you," at first Mom might prompt him ("Say 'Thank you,' Johnnie"), and praise him lavishly when he says it. Once he is responding correctly, she can prompt with "What do you say, Johnnie?" using praise when he says "Thank you." Eventually, she can just comment on it every now and then: "Johnnie, I really like it when you say 'Thank you.'" Indeed, by this time other people may be smiling and complimenting him, and the behavior will be maintained by natural rewards for politeness beyond those from parents.

A Word of Caution: When we talk about a change from rewarding every time to an occasional schedule, this does *not* mean a sudden shift from liberal rewarding to almost none. What it means is a very gradual decline to a level of social rewarding that is still enough to be effective. Just "how much" is a matter of judgment. But keep in mind that too little rewarding means ignoring, and that leads to a possible decline in the behavior. On the other hand, you needn't worry about "too much" rewarding: can you imagine receiving *too many* hugs and smiles (if they are sincere)?

Hopefully, it is obvious in this discussion that we are not talking only of changing a *child's* behavior, for *parents* must change their behavior too, in order to modify the reward *system* and set up the conditions necessary for the child to change.

CHANGING TO OCCASIONAL REWARDS
- AN INEFFECTIVE APPROACH

Mom used tokens, material and social rewards to get Lyn ready on time in the morning. Since the girl had managed it without error for a week, Mom decided to cut down on the rewards. Her mistake was to cut down entirely too fast. As a consequence, Lyn has reverted back to *not being ready on time.*

GRADUALLY CHANGING TO OCCASIONAL REWARDS
- A DIFFERENT APPROACH

This Mom gradually cut back on the material rewards, but maintained the social and token rewards for Gretchen's improved getting-ready behavior. The change to a once-a-week reward may involve some negotiation, but most children will remain motivated by pleasing parents if those parents are good social rewarders. Eventually Mom may also phase out the stars and chart, but should never completely stop giving social rewards for getting ready on time.

Many of the things that we do as adults involve mostly self-rewards. We tell ourselves, "I did a good job on that." We look with satisfaction at our accomplishments, small or large, and congratulate ourselves, or treat ourselves to something special. This self-rewarding is not "automatic," but learned. Some learn it well while others do not seem to learn it at all. Self-rewarding is simply having a good opinion of one's own efforts, and parents can teach this to children by calling attention to their accomplishments, getting the child to verbalize a job well done and express pride in it. "Johnny, you did a great job You can be proud of yourself. Don't you think so? Tell Mommy about the good job you did." Ultimately the self-rewarder still needs social rewards from others, but is not overdependent upon the opinions of others, and values his or her *own* opinion most of all!

11. Clear messages

We can only learn to deal with the world around us if there is some predictability, some degree of reliability about what to expect. It's easy for a parent to be inconsistent. For example, screaming and yelling may be tolerated one day but severely punished the next. Also, one parent may approve of a behavior while the other frowns upon it. Parents are sometimes inconsistent with different children -- one child getting away with something while the other doesn't.

PRINCIPLE 23: It is important that parental approval or disapproval of behavior be consistent and be made clear to the child.

INCONSISTENCY WITH ONE PARENT

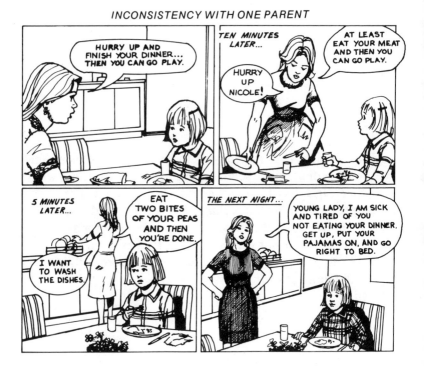

First, Mom told Nicole that she couldn't go play until she finished all her dinner. Yet soon after, Mom backed down and allowed the child to go play after a few bites. This kind of inconsistency teaches Nicole that she really won't have to finish her dinner at all because Mom will eventually change what she said to do. The next night, however, Mom *does* stick with what she said by following through and sending the child to bed for not finishing dinner. Here is a second inconsistency, since one night leaving food on the plate was tolerated while the next night it was punished. From Nicole's point of view the whole experience is confusing and unfair.

CONSISTENCY WITH ONE PARENT
- A BETTER APPROACH

In this example, Mom was specific about what should be done, how long Wanda had to do it, and what would happen if she didn't. No further attention was given. She did not do any reminding or prodding, and finally Mom carried out exactly what she said she would do.

Many dinnertime problems can be avoided if parents observe two rules: do not allow children access to snacks near mealtime, and avoid serving excessive portions of food (especially disliked foods). It is unrealistic to expect a child to "clean the plate" if it is covered with heaps of food.

INCONSISTENCY BETWEEN PARENTS

Mom had a Saturday agreement with Buddy that he must mow the lawn to be able to attend a movie that night. He understood this, yet failed to mow the lawn. Mom was being consistent with their agreement in not allowing him to go to the show. But then Dad "overruled" her and told Buddy he *could* go to the show.

Here we see inconsistency between parents -- the failure of one to support the other. Dad, in this case, gets to play the "good guy" (which automatically makes Mom the "heavy"). The result is that Mom is now angry, and Buddy has learned that he can get around his parents through "divide and conquer." Furthermore, if such inconsistency occurs often, it can put serious strains upon a marriage. Overruling is sometimes used in unhappy marriages as a hostile way for a husband or wife to get at the other. When it occurs for any reason, it undermines parental authority and teaches the child to manipulate adults.

CONSISTENCY BETWEEN PARENTS
- A BETTER APPROACH

Obviously Dad supported Mom in this example and made it clear to Scotty that they are united when it comes to dealing with his behavior. If parents are in disagreement, they may wish to immediately go into *private* conference. Then they can let the child know their joint decision. Neither parent should have the power to "overrule" the other in front of the child without discussion. Nor should one parent reluctantly go along, while making the other out to be a villain. For example, the father would have done this had he said, "It would be OK with me, son, but your mother has already said no." This may be consistency, but it is certainly a "lame-duck" variety.

In our examples we have demonstrated inconsistency with one parent and between parents. There are, of course, many additional variations of inconsistency. For example, a child says to Father, "Mommy said I can have a candy bar." In fact Mom has said no such thing. In such cases, a parent who is not sure should always check.

Another common situation involves having different standards of conduct for different children in the family. One child shouldn't be able to get away with breaking "house rules" while another cannot. No child should get special unearned privileges because of age or sex. (It is, of course, appropriate to allow more mature children certain freedoms which are not yet available to their younger brothers and sisters.) Older children frequently feel angry when younger ones "get away with murder" because "they're too young to know better." Even small children understand basic rules of conduct. A favorite game for older children, is to put younger children "up to something" that will get them into trouble. Consistency in punishment is no virtue if the wrong child is branded the culprit! You cannot, of course, treat each child identically. Nevertheless, make every effort to be consistent!

Finally, think back to our examples involving the lawn and movie. Let's again assume the son and his mother have an agreement that if he mows the lawn he can go to the show that night. Further, suppose that he mows it, does it on time, and does it well. However, later that same afternoon, he gets into some minor trouble with Mom. She becomes very angry, and tells him in no uncertain terms, "That's it! I've had it! No show for you tonight!" In other words, everything is off. Indeed, she may have reason to be angry and to do something about his misbehavior. But this issue has nothing at all to do with the lawn-and-show agreement! Mom has suddenly and perhaps unfairly canceled the entire agreement after her son has completed his part. The right to go to the show was already earned through his efforts in mowing the lawn. Parents need to be willing to carry out their side of a bargain made with their children (just as they would with other adults) if they want to retain credibility. Mom may want to punish her son, but it should not involve the movie.

We understand that it may be difficult for a suddenly-angered parent to watch a child collect a previously earned reward. It is very tempting, when angry, to withdraw *all* good things from a child including previously earned rewards. Yet it is essential in this situation that Mom and Dad "grin and bear it." Parents must stick by their agreements if their word is to mean anything.

There are, of course, extreme situations where an agreement may appropriately be changed. For instance, assume the boy had fulfilled the agreement, but later deliberately injured his sister. Should he still be allowed to go out that evening? Most parents would say "No!" Perhaps a compromise is in order when *serious* misbehavior occurs. Mom might react to the new situation by modifying the agreement: "You completed the lawn, and I owe you a movie for that. But, you also hurt your sister, so you're not going out *tonight.*''

Because we are all human, *absolute* consistency is not possible. Nevertheless, it is very important to avoid ''changing the rules,'' father-mother contradictions, and lack of follow through on agreements. If we expect our children to behave consistently, we need to provide them with good models to follow!

We have emphasized the importance of having a positive focus and looking for good things to reward in others. It is also essential that when we socially reward someone, we do not mix in a social punishment at the same time. It is very easy to do, particularly if you are trying to switch from a negative focus to a positive focus.

PRINCIPLE 24: When parents combine punishment with a reward it is confusing to children. The punishment usually has the most impact, leaving the child with predominantly bad feelings.

The most common form of combining reward with punishment is in the statement, ''I like that, but...'' For example, ''That was a pretty good job, *but* I think you can do better.'' ''I like your new hair style, *but* I think I liked it better when it was longer.'' ''Your room looks a lot better, *but* your closet's still a mess.''

The "but..." offsets the value of the reward, leaving at best a rather shallow social reward. Often, it is no reward at all because the person responds emotionally to the negative aspect of the remark. It's like getting a pat on the back and a kick in the rear at the same time! Compliments and criticisms poured together mix about as well as oil and water.

Compare the next two examples:

REWARDING WITH A MIXED MESSAGE

REWARDING WITHOUT A MIXED MESSAGE

In these two examples Dad has a choice: He can make a big thing out of the good job the boy did with the dishes (positive focus), he can direct his attention toward the water slopped on the floor (negative focus), or he can respond to both. Certainly Dad does not want the boy to spill water on the floor while rinsing dishes, but that is a separate matter from the dishes. What counts is that Tom and Jim did rinse the dishes and put them into the washer. Dad should reward the dishcleaning, as in the second example, without any mixed message. Then he can tend to the clean-up separately. He can also reward the boy for helping with the clean-up.

This principle may seem rather obvious, yet we have found that many people liberally dish out mixed messages while being convinced that they are actually good social rewarders. Good intentions are not sufficient if parents mask punishment in what they consider to be social rewards for their children. It is easy to check yourself as a social rewarder. Take notes (or have someone else take them) and record what you say to others in the way of compliments. See if you add a "but..." If you discover that you are masking punishment in rewards, we say to you, "Congratulations for trying to have a positive focus, but..."

12. Keeping track

How do you really know whether your attempt to change a child's behavior is working? Sometimes it's obvious, but often you don't know -- *unless* you keep records.

If you have pinpointed a behavior and want to begin changing it, it is best to start with information on *how often* it is happening. Mental records or impressions are not enough, for our memories are notoriously faulty. One of the greatest failures in behavior-change programs is not keeping accurate records. Behavior change can be a slow process and, even though it is actually happening, a parent may not be completely aware of it at the time with casual observation.

PRINCIPLE 25: Before trying to change a behavior it is helpful to count the number of times it occurs, usually over a period of a few days.

Once you have pinpointed the troublesome behavior, the following steps should be taken for adequate record keeping:

1. *Redefine [if necessary] the behavior in a positive focus.* It is typically human to see problems in terms of behavior we don't like. But that means we are watching and counting undesirable behavior -- a negative focus. Any negative behavior can be redefined so we can direct our attention toward the positive behavior that should take its place. For example:

The Problem in Negative Focus:	The Problem in Positive Focus:
Wet pants	Dry pants
Hitting brother	Minutes of cooperative play with brother (no hitting)
Not eating everything on plate	Eating everything (or an agreed minimum)
Late	On time
Interrupting adult conversation	Minutes of not interrupting adult conversation
Bad talk (e.g., ''you dummy!'')	Good talk (freedom from bad statements)
Excessive telephone conversations (over a specified length)	Reasonable telephone conversations (within a specified length)
Bed left unmade	Bed made

To express behavior in positive focus is essential because, when we are ready to initiate a change, we want all our efforts, attention, and concern to be directed toward the *desired* behavior. That can only happen with a positive focus. Catch them being good!

2. *Design a method of counting the behavior.* Recall again that it is important to obtain a measure of the behavior *before* anything is done to change it. At this point parents should continue to behave in their normal way. If you are going to deal with dry pants, you need to decide how often to check and over how long a period. Just checking one morning or relying upon your memory is not sufficient. Again, with each measure of behavior, it is important for the parents to continue to relate to the child exactly as before during this "counting" period, thereby providing a normal opportunity for the behavior to occur. For example, if you are checking "dry pants," don't change your child's fluid intake or start taking him or her to the toilet more often. If observing cooperative play, don't provide a new set of toys to play with. When measuring completion of dinner, don't change the types of food served nor the portions given. If you want to see how often someone is on time, don't change the types of situations involved. To get an idea of the frequency that a child interrupts conversing parents, let your conversation patterns remain the same, at the usual places and times.

Some possible methods of counting the positive-focus behaviors listed above are:

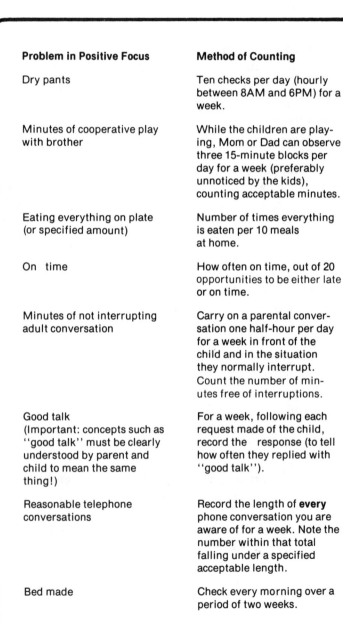

Problem in Positive Focus	Method of Counting
Dry pants	Ten checks per day (hourly between 8AM and 6PM) for a week.
Minutes of cooperative play with brother	While the children are playing, Mom or Dad can observe three 15-minute blocks per day for a week (preferably unnoticed by the kids), counting acceptable minutes.
Eating everything on plate (or specified amount)	Number of times everything is eaten per 10 meals at home.
On time	How often on time, out of 20 opportunities to be either late or on time.
Minutes of not interrupting adult conversation	Carry on a parental conversation one half-hour per day for a week in front of the child and in the situation they normally interrupt. Count the number of minutes free of interruptions.
Good talk (Important: concepts such as "good talk" must be clearly understood by parent and child to mean the same thing!)	For a week, following each request made of the child, record the response (to tell how often they replied with "good talk").
Reasonable telephone conversations	Record the length of **every** phone conversation you are aware of for a week. Note the number within that total falling under a specified acceptable length.
Bed made	Check every morning over a period of two weeks.

3. *Count the behavior.* Use a simple tally sheet and
   record the behavior as it happens, keeping it accurate
   throughout the time specified. Don't try to trust this
   job to your memory alone. Do not show it to the child
   (remember, you are not yet trying to do anything to
   change the behavior). Total it up so you have a
   summary statement for the week or period involved.
   For example, you might find that your child had dry
   pants 32 out of 70 checks (or about 46% of the time).
   Or there might be 14 interruptions during the 3½
   hours of monitored parental conversations that week
   (or 4 per hour). This is the *before* count.

At the end of your attempt to change behavior you will
want to again run an identical measure of the behavior, the
after count. It can then be compared with the *before* count,
to decide whether your efforts have been effective. The
before and *after* behavior counts will be clearly different if
the program had any effect. If there is no difference, then
it's "back to the drawing board." Remember, the problem is
not with you or the child, but with the program you
designed. Try again -- and continue to keep accurate
records!

BROTHER AND SISTER FIGHTING
- AN INEFFECTIVE PLAN FOR BEHAVIOR CHANGE

Brother/sister "fights" are a common family experience. But it is not evident in this example just what Wendy wants to change. In her conversation with Mildred, Wendy was not clear about the behavior to which she objected. What exactly is "fighting"? She did not set up a systematic method of observing the behavior, relying instead on her impressions. Obviously the children cannot be fighting "all the time." (Although we know it can often seem that way!) After her talk with Mildred, Wendy set up a reward system *not connected to any specific behavior* (how does she decide which nights to give dessert?). And finally, since she had no accurate *before and after* behavior count, she did not know whether her effort *really* worked or not. Maybe it worked. But maybe it didn't. She doesn't *know*.

BROTHER AND SISTER FIGHTING
- A DIFFERENT PLAN FOR BEHAVIOR CHANGE

Here Mary has pinpointed a desired behavior (in a positive focus) by defining it in an observable and countable way. She is in the process of measuring how often it occurs *before* attempting to do anything about it. Her friend Jan expresses the feeling of urgency many of us experience when we want to change a disruptive behavior in our children. We want to get it changed immediately and not take time to collect and record information about it. But Mary wisely is going to take that time, tolerate the behavior just a little longer, and this will serve as a solid basis from which to begin her behavior change effort.

Keeping careful records of behavior is hard work and often takes valuable time that could be used for other things. It is tempting and easy to "slack off" and just try to keep track of behavior mentally. Unfortunately it rarely if ever works! Written records made immediately after the behavior occurs *will* tell you whether your efforts to change behavior are working, and to what degree. There will be no vague statements like "maybe it works" or "it seems to be helping." Only after you have pinpointed the behavior *and* recorded how often it is happening, are you ready to most effectively set out to change the behavior.

13. The family that works together...

Imagine this situation: Mom and Dad have two young children. At the end of his work day, Dad comes home, hoping to watch the 6 o'clock news. The kids are running about, making a lot of noise. Dad calls out to Mom in the other room, "You're home with these kids all the time. Can't you do something about this noise? I work all day and I'd like to come home just once in a while and have a little peace and quiet." This father believes that it is Mom's primary responsiblity to make sure the children are quiet when he is there.

In a minor variation of the same theme, Mom may come home from work and hear Dad say, "These kids have been a terror today, and I want you to do something about it!" He believes that Mom has responsibility to dish out the punishment and may have threatened the children with, "Just wait until your mother gets home!"

Some parents believe that "boy problems" are Dad's responsibility while "girl problems" are Mom's. Mother says, "Can't you do something with that son of *yours*?" Father suggests, "You better have a talk with *your* daughter." Such division of parental responsibility is inefficient for dealing with child problems. We advocate an equal relationship, with shared roles and responsibilities.

> **PRINCIPLE 26: All members of the family should be involved in changing a child's behavior.**

A family is built upon a complex system of interactions among parents, children, and often relatives. It should be apparent that a child's behavior is unlikely to change if only one family member modifies his or her reactions while the others continue on as before. If we want any behavior change program to be effective, it must include all members of the family, making clear what part they play in the situation, what they must do, and how they must change. Everybody can be involved in the planning by sitting down together and talking it over, so that everyone knows what is going on.

Consider this dinner scene:

CUTTING CALORIES
- INEFFECTIVE FAMILY INVOLVEMENT

Becky needs to lose weight and the other family members are certainly involved. The trouble here is that they are also penalized by having to miss favorite desserts. No attempt was made to include the family in a positive focus upon better eating habits. In fact, her younger brother takes delight in having a negative focus as he throws a barb and points out a continuing poor eating habit.

CUTTING CALORIES
- EFFECTIVE FAMILY INVOLVEMENT

In this example, the eating habits of the other family members are not affected by Betty's diet. They are not penalized because one person has a weight problem. Also, the group is encouraged to help Betty with her eating and not sabotage her efforts. Unserved food is removed from the table so Betty is less tempted to have second helpings. She is given a choice of staying at the table and watching the others eat chocolate cake or going to another room (which might be less painful if she really wants cake). Finally, Dad makes a point of encouraging her. The 10-year-old younger brother said nothing directly to Betty. This may be the best support one can realistically expect from a younger brother. (If the younger brother did continue to throw barbs and tease his sister, Mom might want to deal directly with his teasing by making *his* dessert an earned reward for not teasing during dinner).

Weight loss is a slow process. Pounds do not suddenly disappear, and any person changing eating habits needs all the encouragement possible. With all family members involved and on a positive focus, there can be lots of social rewards for exercising, eating smaller portions, and giving up high-calorie foods.

Thus, regardless of the behavior to be changed, you need to be sure that all family members are involved, know how to socially reward the desired behavior, and follow through. Treat it as a family project where nobody feels excluded. It is particularly important that no family member be penalized by a program to change another's behavior, since a likely reaction to an undeserved penalty is to sabotage the program.

☺

How do you get other children in the family to cooperate with a behavior change program, rather than ridicule the child involved or sabotage parents' efforts? It's no secret that children enjoy teasing and razzing each other, and may even take delight when the other one gets in trouble with parents. In short, kids can develop an acute sense of negative focus by eagerly picking away at anything they know will irritate a brother or sister. The end result is that Mom or Dad play referee. When dealing with a specific behavior problem, we want to be sure that not only Mom and Dad, but also brother or sister, have a positive focus on the improved behavior. Reward sharing provides a reason for the other child to encourage behavior change rather than hinder it.

> **PRINCIPLE 27: One way to include members of the family in changing a child's behavior is through reward sharing: everybody experiences something nice as a result of the child's success.**

Choosing the reward to share must be done carefully. It has to be something that everybody likes and it must be special -- that is, something which doesn't occur very often. In other words, *it is not already a regular part of family entertainment.* If it's routine to go for pizza every Friday night, don't suddenly insist that one child has to "shape up" or nobody gets to go. That puts everybody in the position of being punished if the child in question does not immediately perform well. It may result in great pressure from brothers or sisters who don't want to be cheated out of their normal fun. Once the special family reward has been selected, behavior is then recorded and socially rewarded, step-by-step. Possibly points or stars can be used until a desired goal is reached. Then the family gets to share the special reward.

The emphasis is not upon *if* the goal is going to be reached, but *when.* Parents should also avoid planning shared rewards that are *time limited*, running out at a certain date and placing a child under pressure ("If James gets 50 points *by Sunday*, we can all take a ride to the beach."). Instead, it should be planned to allow the child to achieve success at his or her own pace ("*When* James has collected 50 points, we can all plan a trip to the beach.").

TAKING CARE OF PETS - INEFFECTIVE REWARD SHARING

TAKING CARE OF PETS - EFFECTIVE REWARD SHARING

In the example on page 153, Dad set up a shared reward for the boys and specified the behavior required, but expected a perfect record by the next weekend. When Wayne carries out his task for three out of five days, he gets no reward for his partial success. Dick is completely faithful to the task, yet he too gets no reward. Dad set it up so that any failure on Wayne's part would automatically result in punishment for both boys, regardless of how well Dick did his job. Conflict between the two boys can certainly be expected.

David's Dad, in the second example, sets up a shared reward system for both boys. No one is left out, and both are earning points toward separate family goals. Dad has set no time limit, so he rewards *any* improvement in David's efforts. The boys know that eventually they'll be going to a show. Also, Joel is likely to show more interest in David's success and may even remind him to take care of his pet. Remember, in a good reward sharing plan, you must be sure that the kids are indeed sharing rewards and not being punished through denial of an expected reward. Keep in mind that rewards are an individual thing. With children of very different ages you may have to do some searching for a reward that interests *everybody*! It is certainly desirable to ask, and to talk over with the children what rewards would make everybody happy.

Besides being helpful in changing one child's behavior, there are also broader family benefits of reward sharing. There is a shift toward a more positive focus and away from a "failure" orientation. In addition, such joint efforts tend to give the family a sense of unity through working together.

14. The spice of life

Almost everyone likes to be told "I love you" by someone special. But if that is said 100 times a day, it's going to lose meaning and value. Similarly, a child may consider raisins to be a favorite treat, yet they would cease to be of interest if Mom gives out a pound of them during the course of the day! Parents should keep in mind a wide variety of possible rewards to use with their children.

> **PRINCIPLE 28: All children like reward variety. Nobody enjoys the same thing all the time. Some rewards can be overused so that effectiveness is lost.**

Some of the more popular rewards are listed on the following page. You can add to the list for a specific child.

A "STARTER LIST" OF REWARDS FOR CHILDREN

Social Rewards	Token Rewards	Material Rewards	Activities
Attention	Stars	Candy or cookies	Bicycling
Winks	Points		Movies
		Raisins	
Looks of surprise or joy	Drawings of happy faces	Popcorn	Bowling
			Picnicking
Smiles	Grades	Ice Cream	
			Swimming
Verbal praise	Poker chips	Small toys	
			TV time
Hugs	Cards	Clothes	
			Special privileges
Kisses	Play money	Games	
Affectionate touch	Money	Money	

One of the reasons token rewards are so useful with children is that they allow for so much variety. Money, clearly "material," is also really the supreme "token" of all! For adults or children, it can be exchanged for any of the valued material things in life. Likewise, points, poker chips, or stars can be cashed in for various children's rewards.

When trying to get some additional reward variety in day-to-day activities, one approach for parents (perhaps an obvious one) is simply to *ask* children what kinds of things they enjoy or would like to earn. It may happen that older children will say, "Oh, I don't know, I can't think of anything." Parents can get around this seemingly low interest by carefully observing their children and noting what kinds of things they spend their spare time doing. You can assume these are things they enjoy. Write down these activities and then allow children to earn *time* for them: For example, if a son spends a lot of time watching TV, use that time as a reward for studying. If a daughter enjoys bicycle riding, let her earn time for the trips to a bike trail. If a child is excited over shopping on Saturday with the weekly allowance, let that allowance be earned by correctly doing daily chores. Keep in mind a child's wide variety of enjoyed activities. You can make those activities dependent upon desired behavior.

A question often raised on this approach is, "Isn't this a little like tricking the child -- making an activity they already like into a new reward?" Nothing is secret or hidden in this approach. Everything is to be clearly explained to the child. The only thing new is in requiring that behavior be reward-oriented. The alternative is for the child to engage in all the enjoyed activities *without* doing necessary chores (or whatever behavior is involved), and then have parents nag and perhaps even punish. That approach isn't likely to win any prizes for effectiveness! It's far better for a child to do chores *first*, and *then* earn the right to engage in enjoyed activities -- free of parental nagging or punishment. Making rewards dependent upon desired behavior teaches a child responsibility, a valuable lesson for later life.

We've all had the experience of being "burned" because a verbal agreement is later remembered very differently by the people involved. Memories being notoriously faulty, adult agreements or transactions often require written documents. Similarly, child-adult agreements within the home can be "spelled-out" in writing.

> **PRINCIPLE 29: Parents and children can form a contract, a written or picture document that specifies the desired behaviors and the rewards for each.**

The purpose of a contract is to provide a document which clearly specifies the behavior expected and the rewards that can be earned. It is written in simple language (or pictures for small children), is displayed publicly, and helps the parties involved remember the terms of the agreement. Often such a contract is posted somewhere in easy view and used for recording daily behavior change, such as earning gold stars or points. With young kids, parents usually set up a contract on the basis of what they already know about rewards for their children. With older youngsters, parents may need to negotiate a contract -- that is specifying what they want the children to do, exploring what the kids would like to earn, and agreeing upon a fair system of behavior and rewards.

Parents may have to spend considerable time with the children in negotiation because of disagreements about the value of rewards (kids sometimes are unrealistic about the cost of material things), and the amount of effort that should go into earning them. Like management and labor, parents and children can usually reach an agreement and can finally "sign" the document to show good faith. If the terms of the contract are carried out by the child, parents need to follow through on their end of the bargain. If either party cannot abide by the agreement, the contract is terminated and a new one drawn up. It is usually best to make a contract only for a short period of time (a week or two), since experience may find it to be too easy or too difficult.

Even the best contracts have to be reevaluated every now and then. Having a written contract is valuable because it requires a positive focus, serves as a visual reminder of the agreement, and keeps both parents and children on target.

A CONTRACT FOR A YOUNG CHILD

In carrying out such a contract, Mom may wish to check the room with Sally in the afternoon just before her regular snack time. She already knows Sally likes cookies, chocolate milk, and fruit. Yet, it may be necessary to prompt Sally at first, re-explain and model how to do each of the things shown in the pictorial contract, using the step-by-step principle. After a couple of days, Sally should be able to manage without further instruction, depending upon her age and physical skills (and upon the degree of perfection Mom expects!).

A CONTRACT FOR AN OLDER BOY

BEHAVIOR	TIME CHECKED	POINTS POSSIBLE	POINTS EARNED						
			MON.	TUE.	WED.	THU.	FRI.	SAT.	SUN.
FEED DOG, FRESH WATER	8 AM	1							
BED MADE	8 AM	1							
HAIR COMBED	TWICE A DAY	2							
TABLE CLEARED	8 PM	2							
GARBAGE TAKEN OUT	8 PM	2							
EVENING HOURS FREE OF INSULTS TO SISTER	HOURLY 6 TO 10	4							
	DAILY TOTAL								
	WEEKLY TOTAL								

REWARD COSTS	POINTS
MOVIE (FAMILY)	40
ROLLER SKATE (FAMILY)	40
OUT FOR PIZZA	40
HAVING FRIEND OVERNIGHT	20
MAKE A DESSERT	20
CHOICE OF TV PROGRAMS FOR ONE EVENING	10

SPECIAL REWARD
WHEN A TOTAL OF 150 POINTS
HAVE BEEN EARNED,
YOU CAN HAVE A PARTY.

SIGNED (PARENT)

SIGNED   (SON)

A number of assumptions are included in this example of a contract. First, the boy must know exactly what the behaviors call for (such as "bed made" or "table cleared"). Second, the parents will have to decide which are the more important behaviors to them and which seem to be the easiest. Points are then weighted accordingly. We are also assuming that the sister who is being "insulted" is able to positive focus and determine, on an hourly basis, whether she was insulted or not. (The *problem behavior* is "insults," which are easy to count, but that would be negative focus. The sister must be able to record time *without* such insults so that the family may reward it.).

In the sample contract, the boy gets a choice of how to cash in earned points. There is a long-term "special reward" included so that after 150 total points are earned a party can be given. Such events happen occasionally in most families anyway, so why not include a party for a special reward? The chart shows daily progress and steps toward the big reward. If the child is doing a good job on most items, the parents may allow self-monitoring (or self-scoring) and posting of points (with occasional checks for accuracy). The whole thing runs out about three weeks later (an older child may be able to handle this longer period), and may be renegotiated at that time if necessary.

Remember, in forming a contract:
1. Pinpoint the desired behavior.
2. Whenever appropriate, state the checking time when the behavior has to be completed. Just saying "feed the dog daily" could mean any time within 24 hours.
3. State behaviors with a positive focus.
4. Clearly specify what the rewards are, their cost, and when they will be given.
5. Place the contract in a public place for all to see. Most kids really like earning things and seeing their

progress publicly displayed.

6. Re-evaluate the contract on a weekly basis to
   determine effectiveness. If necessary, new reward
   values can be assigned to desired behaviors. For
   example, if a behavior is not occurring at all, the
   reward may be too small and can be raised.

Contracts are a common means of adult communication.
They require both parties to be clear about their desires and
expectations, and they specify both payoffs for successful
completion and penalties for failure. If we are to improve our
communication with children, such clear statements can be
of great value. Although a written contract is not always
necessary (just as it is not always necessary between adults)
it does allow for fewer misunderstandings. Also, a written
contract says to both parties "We are serious about
changing things here!"

15. Relax, nobody's perfect!

A young mother was recently in our office describing what it is like to be divorced, working full-time, and trying to raise three children (ages 3, 7, and 9). She looked haggard as she sighed, "I've tried everything I know -- yes, even behavior modification, but that didn't work. The kids are at each other, fighting and yelling, talking back to me, and I don't have a moment's peace." She began to cry, then described in more detail the constant turmoil in her home. Her own efforts went unappreciated, and a great deal of friction among all of them made each day a hassle.

This mother had a tremendous responsibility and felt she couldn't keep on functioning without some freedom from chaos at home. She said she had "tried behavior modification" so we inquired further. She had made an effort but not a very efficient one. It seems she had designed a reward system based upon a negative focus and had failed to include any step-by-step planning. Furthermore, she had allowed her whole effort at changing things only one week to succeed. When nothing changed, she gave up.

> **PRINCIPLE 30: Considerable time and effort are needed for behavior change. Each of us has spent a lifetime learning to become the way we are. One shouldn't expect people to change overnight.**

The young mother described above needed help in obtaining accurate behavior counts and making a number of revisions in her behavior-change program. We encouraged her to try again, but this time she was urged to stick with it for at least a month. She reported back to us each week on how it was going. Her summary reports:

First week: Not much difference.

Second week: The only marked change is that John isn't screaming so much. He talks in a normal voice more often.

Third week: The two oldest kids are getting along better. There has been a reduction in fights.

Fourth week: Maybe this approach is going to work after all! Four of the six desired behaviors are really changed. There's a better atmosphere at home.

Changing a single small behavior in one person can be quite a task. Imagine the complexity of behaviors this mother had to deal with!

It is only natural to want fast results in dealing with troublesome behavior, but that desire must not keep us from working realistically. Recall the ignoring principle? (page 67). Just as we may have to ignore an undesirable behavior repeatedly, so we may have to pay careful attention and lavishly reward a behavior we like hundreds of times before we consider it completely satisfactory. We may need to experiment, revise and change contracts, juggle points around, rephrase wording, and renegotiate with older kids. As we have stated before, all this is hard work for any parent and can test one's patience when there is no overnight dramatic change. Our advice is to stay with it at least a month, once you think you have a good program. If it's still not working -- remember, it's not the *child's fault*. It's not *your fault*. It's a *faulty program*! That means back to the drawing board and some more thought.

It's a reality of life that as children get older, they fall more and more under the influence of social reward systems outside the home and family. Their friends, their school, and their activities may command much more of their interest than do parents, family, or events in the home. This means that parents have less and less direct effect upon their children's behavior. As youngsters grow up it is no longer easy to restrict access to prized rewards and choose the appropriate behavior to earn them. Sometimes parents experience these changes with a feeling of helplessness, worrying about their children and then blaming themselves if the children get into trouble ("Where did I go wrong?"). A parent cannot feel responsible for everything a child does because there are other strong influences upon any child's behavior. Also, a parent cannot expect to have as much effect upon a maturing teenager as upon a 5-year-old!

Parents may have to watch teenagers grow away from them somewhat and do many things not liked. Also, they may be unable to do much of anything about it! The boys' hair-length struggle of the 60's and 70's is a classic example. A teenage boy may be far more influenced by the social rewards from his buddies and girlfriends than by the approval of Mom or Dad. If his girlfriend likes long hair, that is probably what the boy will wear. When parents realize that their approval and social rewards have lost some influence, they sometimes attempt to use coercion with teenagers and become bogged down in power struggles. In the long run such struggles cannot improve the family relationship, and may poison the later establishment of a rewarding adult-to-adult relationship between parents and their grownup children.

Parents *can* relate positively with children approaching adulthood and not lay guilt upon themselves by assuming everything the child does is their "fault." With adulthood,

most children will come to a new appreciation for their
parents' company, interest, and approval, but on an
adult-to-adult basis.

Throughout this book we have tried to make clear that
being a parent is hard work and a great responsibility. With
consistent effort and positive involvement it can also be a
joyful experience. These 30 behavioral principles, when
systematically used, can produce major improvements in
family life, both for parents and children. Parents are happy
when their children succeed and can be praised. Children
are happiest when parents are pleased with them -- smiling,
hugging, and laughing, rather than frowning, nagging, and
punishing.

Don't get discouraged if you find yourself having difficulty
applying these principles consistently. All of us are human --
nobody's perfect! No one can expect to do "the right thing"
all the time. Even if some "all-knowing" psychologist were
to lay down the ABSOLUTE RULES for how one should raise
children to be PERFECT, no human being (including the
psychologist) could follow them all the time!

We hope this book has been interesting and helpful to
you. Our thirty principles, although not new or
"revolutionary," suggest a turnabout in some of the ways
that parents often relate to children.

Our message is both simple and complex. Each person's
sense of well being, enjoyment of the good life, and

self-worth, all depend upon understanding and gaining some control over the consequences of his or her actions. And it is as true for parents as it is for children.

We are actually talking about a lifestyle, a way of relating to children *and* adults, in which we look for the good things in ourselves and others, and purposely develop them. People grow when we socially reward often, ignore what we don't like, and punish sparingly if at all. And remember that people don't change instantly! We all need encouragement as we improve a bit at a time. Such a lifestyle includes consistency instead of chaos, a focus on today rather than tomorrow or yesterday, and an active sharing with others of a world rich in variety and warm relationships.

The benefits go far beyond the immediate improvement in behavior. Children who are raised with a positive focus and lots of social rewards learn to relate to others in the same way. Their friendships during the developing years will be enhanced, and their adult intimate relations and perhaps interactions with children of their own will be based upon this positive approach. They also learn to reward themselves and to be successful in achieving their own goals. There is no better definition of self-sufficiency and happiness!

A LIST OF THE THIRTY PRINCIPLES USED IN THIS BOOK

1. Labels -- such as "hyperactive," "aggressive," or "insecure" -- really don't explain behavior, nor do they give parents guidance in how to deal with their children.

2. Behavior is influenced by two major factors: heredity and learning.

3. Most human behavior is learned. Children learn both desirable and undesirable behavior in the same way.

4. All people, including children, behave differently depending upon where they are and whom they are with.

5. We keep doing things which are followed by good consequences or good feelings (rewards).

6. We stop doing things which are followed by bad consequences, bad feelings, or no rewards.

7. Our learning experiences determine when we feel such natural emotions as love, elation, anxiety, and sadness.

8. Because each person is unique, rewards must also be unique -- that is, "tailor-made" to fit the individual.

9. We all like material rewards such as money, food, or toys. But it is really social rewards like attention, praise, and affection that make us feel good about ourselves.

10. Attention is one of the most powerful social rewards, for both desirable and undesirable behavior. Even scolding a child is paying attention, and may be rewarding!

11. Much of our behavior is learned by imitating the people around us, particularly parents.

12. Parents need not worry about giving "too much" love and affection. The way to "spoil" a child is to reward undesirable behavior.

13. Children will not continue to do things (such as chores) just because parents say "you ought" or "I told you to;" there must also be some good consequence (reward).

14. People who give many social rewards to others tend to receive the same in return.

15. One way to eliminate an undesirable behavior is to consistently and permanently ignore it -- never reward it, even with attention.

16. It is rewarding to experience a sense of relief when we avoid or escape something unpleasant.

17. Punishment is a way of stopping an undesirable behavior that simply cannot be ignored. If punishment is to be used, it must be clearly related to the behavior, given immediately, of low to moderate intensity, and certain to occur.

18. It is preferable that parents have a "positive focus," actively looking for good behavior in their children and rewarding it.

19. To change behavior, it is first necessary to "pinpoint" -- that is, identify the behavior in question so that it can be both observed and counted.

20. Learning a new behavior is a step-by-step process. Generally, the smaller the steps, the easier the learning.

21. Ideal timing for rewarding a child is immediately following the desired behavior. The longer the delay between behavior and reward, the less the effect upon learning.

22. There are two basic schedules of rewarding: every time and occasionally. It is best to start by rewarding the desired behavior every time it occurs. Eventually a parent can change to an occasional schedule.

23. It is important that parental approval or disapproval of behavior be consistent and be made clear to the child.

24. When parents combine punishment with a reward it is confusing to children. The punishment usually has the most impact, leaving the child with predominantly bad feelings.

25. Before trying to change a behavior, it is helpful to count the number of times it occurs, usually over a period of a few days.

26. All members of the family should be involved in changing a child's behavior.

27. One way to include members of the family in changing a child's behavior is through reward sharing: everybody experiences something nice as a result of the child's success.

28. All children like reward variety. Nobody enjoys the same thing all the time. Some rewards can be overused so that effectiveness is lost.

29. Parents and children can form a contract, a written or picture document that specifies the desired behaviors and the rewards for each.

30. Considerable time and effort are needed for behavior change. Each of us has spent a lifetime learning to become the way we are. One shouldn't expect people to change overnight.

CHECKLIST FOR A BEHAVIOR CHANGE PROGRAM

1. Identify a behavior. Preferably work with one or two relatively simple ones rather than a whole set.

2. Define the behavior (pinpoint) so that it can be *observed* and *counted*.

3. Rephrase any definition from a negative focus to a positive one.

4. Observe and count the behavior as it is currently happening without changing anything. Do this for at least a week.

5. Devise a system of rewards that are most likely to work for that person -- especially social rewards.

6. Explain to the child and other family members the plan.

7. Implement the plan, being sure to be consistent, rewarding immediately, and using reward variety.

8. Shape the behavior by rewarding step-by-step toward the final goal.

9. Stay with it for a pre-determined period of time, measured in weeks, not days.

10. Keep counting the behavior and note progress. Revise your plan if necessary.

FURTHER READINGS

On Parenting

Eimers, R., and Aitchison, R. *Effective Parents/Responsible Children.* New York: McGraw-Hill, 1978.

Patterson, G. *Families: Application of Social Learning to Family Life.* Champaign, Illinois: Research Press, 1975.

Patterson, G. *Living With Children.* Champaign, Illinois: Research Press, 1971.

Zifferblatt, S. *Improving Study and Homework Behaviors.* Champaign, Illinois: Research Press, 1970.

On Being Married

Belliveau, F., and Richter, L. *Understanding Human Sexual Inadequacy.* New York: Little, Brown, 1970, (Bantam Books Edition, 1971).

Knox, D.E. *Dr. Knox's Marital Exercise Book.* New York: David McKay, 1975.

For Children

Palmer, P. *Liking Myself.* San Luis Obispo, California: Impact Publishers, 1977.

Palmer, P. *The Mouse, the Monster, and Me.* San Luis Obispo, California: Impact Publishers, 1977.

For Teens

Gnagey, T. *How to Put Up With Parents.* Facilitation House.

On Personal Growth

Alberti, R.E., and Emmons, M.L. *Your Perfect Right: A Guide to Assertive Behavior.* San Luis Obispo, California: Impact Publishers, 1970, 1974, 1978.

Ellis, A., and Harper, R. *A New Guide to Rational Living.* New York: Prentice-Hall, 1975.

Hamachek, D.E. *Encounters With the Self.* New York: Holt, Rinehart and Winston, 1971, 1978.

Phelps, S., and Austin, N. *The Assertive Woman.* San Luis Obispo, California: Impact Publishers, 1975.

For Serious Students

Watson, D., and Tharp, R. *Self-Directed Behavior.* Monterey, California: Brooks-Cole, 1972.

Whaley, D., and Malott, R. *Elementary Principles of Behavior.* New York: Appleton-Century-Crofts, 1971.

— *Serving Human Development Since 1970* —

We hope you have enjoyed reading this book.
For more books with "IMPACT" we invite you
to order the following titles. . .

YOUR PERFECT RIGHT
A Guide to Assertive Living [5th Edition]
by Robert E. Alberti, Ph.D. and
Michael L. Emmons, Ph.D.

THE assertiveness classic, now updated and completely rewritten. New chapters on assertive sexuality, assertiveness at work, goal-setting, and more. Expanded material on anger, relationships, anxiety management. Totally revised, this FIFTH EDITION has more than double the material of the original 1970 edition.
Softcover $7.95/Hardcover $11.95 Book No. 07-0

THE ASSERTIVE WOMAN
A New Look
by Stanlee Phelps, M.S.W. and
Nancy Austin, M.B.A.

Completely revised and updated second edition of the classic. Over a quarter-million copies of the original provided inspiration and encouragement to women and groups. New expanded discussions of careers, individuality, children, relationships (lovers, family, friends), and more.
Softcover $8.95 Book No. 61-5

REBUILDING
When Your Relationship Ends
by Bruce Fisher, Ed.D.

A book for those who are putting their lives back together after divorce or after other crises. Rebuilding includes aids for coping with the fifteen "building blocks" that mark the path to recovery: denial, loneliness, guilt, rejection, grief, anger, letting go, self-concept, friendships, leftover love, trust, sexuality, responsibility, singleness and freedom.
Softcover $8.95 Book No. 30-5

THE COUPLE'S JOURNEY
Intimacy as a Path to Wholeness
by Susan M. Campbell, Ph.D.

"Coupling, like life, is a continually changing process." Dr.Campbell guides us on the five-stage path of growth traveled by every intimate relationship: romance, power struggle, stability, commitment and co-creation. Here is help in discovering new meaning in the often confusing process of living intimately with another person.
Softcover $7.95 Book No. 45-3

PLAYFAIR
Everybody's Guide to Non-Competitive Play
by Matt Weinstein, Ph.D. and
Joel Goodman, Ed.D.

Now you can play games where EVERYONE wins! Sixty non-competitive games for large and small groups, adults, young adults, schools, children, families. Detailed descriptions with complete instructions for "play-leaders." A delightful book that takes play seriously and makes it a way of life; filled with playful photographs!
Softcover $9.95 Book No. 50-X

SURVIVING WITH KIDS
A Lifeline for Overwhelmed Parents
by Wayne Bartz, Ph.D. and
Richard Rasor, Ed.D.

A jargon-free, practical book for parents! Thirty proven principles of behavior applied to parent-child interaction. Clearly written, down-to-earth, and delightfully illustrated with cartoon-style examples of everyday situations. A solid guide for first-time parents and those who sometimes feel overwhelmed... and isn't that everybody?
Softcover $7.95 Book No. 55-0

DON'T SWEAT THE SMALL STUFF
P.S. It's All Small Stuff
by Michael R. Mantell, Ph.D.

Collection of short articles from a well-known media psychologist on dozens of life problems: alcohol, anxiety, divorce, drugs, illness, parenting, relationships...more. Written in popular, friendly style, yet based on the latest psychological research.
Softcover $8.95 Book No. 56-9

NO MORE SECRETS
Protecting Your Child from Sexual Assault
by Caren Adams and Jennifer Fay

A supportive, conversational guide for parents who wish to teach their young children how to prevent sexual advances. Points out that most offenders are not strangers but relatives and "friends." This important resource encourages open discussion — "no secrets" — between parents and children. Dialogue, games and other tools to help parents instruct children 3 and up.
Softcover $4.95 Book No. 24-0

LIKING MYSELF
by Pat Palmer, Ed.D.
Illustrated by Betty Shondeck

A child-size introduction to concepts of feelings, self-esteem and assertiveness for youngsters 5-9. Delightful drawings help convey its message to young readers. Liking Myself is widely used by parents and teachers to help children learn and appreciate the good things about themselves, their feelings and their behavior.
Softcover $4.95; w/Teacher guide $6.45
Book No. 41-0

THE MOUSE, THE MONSTER & ME!
Assertiveness for Young People
by Pat Palmer, Ed.D.
Illustrated by Betty Shondeck

Assertiveness concepts for youngsters 8 and up explained in an entertaining way. Non-assertive "mice" and aggressive "monsters" offer young persons an opportunity to develop a sense of personal rights and responsibilities, to become appropriately assertive and to gain a greater sense of self-worth.
Softcover $4.95; w/Teacher Guide $6.45
Book No. 43-7

STRESSMAP: Finding Your Pressure Points
by Michele Haney, Ph.D. and
Edmond Boenisch, Ph.D.

A personal guidebook for pinpointing sources of stress — and finding stress relief! Questionnaire "maps" help readers survey people, money, work, body, mind and leisure stress areas. New second edition devotes chapter to recognizing, preventing and treating burnout. Worksheets permit an individualized plan for relief.
Softcover $7.95 Book No. 60-7

LEAD ON! The Complete Handbook For Group Leaders
by Leslie G. Lawson, Ph.D.,
Franklyn Donant, M.A.,and John Lawson, Ed.D.

Comprehensive guide for leaders of volunteer groups. Twenty-four easy to follow chapters make it easy to lead. Describes essentials for novices and experienced leaders. Indispensable for leaders of youth clubs, church programs, and other "new volunteerism" organizations.
Softcover $7.95 Book No. 27-5

THE STOP SMOKING BOOK
by Margaret Kraker McKean

Lends a gentle helping hand to smokers who have chosen to quit. Humor and humanness — no lectures or shock treatment. Twenty-five personalized Ways lend warm support to "the choice to be stronger than cigarettes."
Softcover $6.95 Book No. 59-3

Please see the following page for more books and information on how to order.

— *Impact* Publishers —

... more books with "IMPACT"

BEYOND THE POWER STRUGGLE
Dealing With Conflict in Love and Work
by Susan M. Campbell, Ph.D.

Explores relationship issues from the viewpoint that, "Differences are inevitable, but conflict and struggle are not." Helps expand perspectives on relationships in love and at work. Psychologist Campbell challenges us to see both sides of a conflict by seeing both sides of ourselves. A creative and thoughtful analysis, accompanied by specific exercises to help relationships grow.
Softcover $8.95   Book No. 46-1

NO IS NOT ENOUGH
Helping Teenagers Avoid Sexual Assault
by Caren Adams, Jennifer Fay and
Jan Loreen-Martin

Guidebook for parents provides proven, realistic strategies to help teens avoid victimization: acquaintance rape, exploitation by adults, touching, influence of media, peer pressures. Includes a primer on what to say and when. Tells how to provide teens with information they need to recognize compromising situations and skills they need to resist pressure.
Softcover $7.95   Book No. 35-6

WORKING FOR PEACE: A Handbook of Practical Psychology And Other Tools
Neil Wollman, Ph.D., Editor

Thirty-five chapter collection of guidelines, ideas and suggestions for improving effectiveness of peace work activities for individuals and groups. Written by psychologists and other experts in communication, speech, and political science.
Softcover $9.95   Book No. 37-2

MARITAL MYTHS: Two Dozen Mistaken Beliefs That Can Ruin A Marriage [Or Make A Bad One Worse]
by Arnold A. Lazarus, Ph.D.

Twenty-four myths of marriage are exploded by a world-reknowned psychologist/marital therapist who has treated hundreds of relationships in over 25 years of practice. Full of practical examples and guidance for self-help readers who want to improve their own marriages.
Softcover $6.95   Book No. 51-8

WHEN MEN ARE PREGNANT
Needs and Concerns of Expectant Fathers
by Jerrold Lee Shapiro, Ph.D.

The first in-depth guide for men who are "expecting." Based on interviews with over 200 new fathers. Covers the baby decision, stages of pregnancy, physical and emotional factors, childbirth, and the first six weeks of fatherhood.
Softcover $8.95   Book No. 62-3

KNOWING WHEN TO QUIT
by Jack Barranger, M.A.

Guide to getting out of counter-productive situations in work, relationships. Quitting can be a courageous act. Helps reader evaluate what's really going on in a situation, formulate options, and make a well-considered decision to stay or quit.
Softcover $8.95   Book No. 57-7

TEEN ESTEEM: A Self-Direction Manual for Young Adults
by Pat Palmer, Ed.D. with   *NEW!*
Melissa Alberti Froehner

Emphasizes self-esteem and self-direction for teens who need refusal skills and positive attitudes to handle peer pressure, substance abuse, sexual expression, other teen problems. Easy to read, evaluated by teens and shaped by their feedback. Cartoon illustrations.
Softcover $6.95   Book No. 66-6

WHAT DO I DO WHEN...? A Handbook for Parents and Other Beleaguered Adults
by Juliet V. Allen, M.A.

"A parent's hotline in handbook." Ready-reference answers to over 50 childrearing dilemmas. Comprehensive, practical, common-sense solutions that really work. Short on theory, long on practical solutions to crying, fighting, bedwetting, car behavior, self-esteem, shyness, working parents, discipline, and much, much more.
Softcover $8.95   Book No. 23-2

TRUST YOURSELF— You Have The Power: A Holistic Handbook for Self-Reliance
by Tony Larsen, D. Min.

Dr. Larsen, teacher, counselor and Unitarian-Universalist minister, demonstrates how each of us has the power to handle our world. This can be done in a completely natural way and depends only upon the power which we already possess.
Softcover $8.95   Book No. 18-6

THE LOVING PARENT: A Guide To Growing Up Before Your Children Do
by Blaize Clement Stewart, M.A.

Offers warm and knowledgeable advice on the joys and jolts of parenthood. Obedience, Manners, Meals, Honesty, Stealing, Cheating, ... Help for parents in balancing their needs with those of their children.
Softcover $8.95   Book No. 63-1

YOU CAN BEAT DEPRESSION
A Guide To Recovery   *NEW!*
by John Preston, Psy.D.

Concise, readable... offers easy access to help for people in need. Clinical psychologist guides readers in self-assessment and how to use appropriate self-help or find professional treatment. An authoritative guide for every depressed person, and anybody who cares about one.
Softcover $8.95   Book No.64-X

GETTING APART TOGETHER: The Couple's Guide to a Fair Divorce or Separation
by Martin Kranitz, M.A.

Couples can save time, money, heartache by preparing their own fair settlement before they see an attorney. Procedures for cooperative negotiation of co-parenting, custody, property, support, insurance, finances, taxes. Includes agendas, forms.
Softcover $8.95   Book No. 58-5

SEND FOR OUR FREE CATALOG

Impact Publishers' books are available at booksellers throughout the U.S.A. and in many other countries. If you are not able to find a title of interest at a nearby bookstore, we would be happy to fill your direct order. Please send us:
1. Complete name, address and zip code information
2. The full title and book no.'s of the book(s) you want
3. The number of copies of each book
4. California residents add 6-1/4% sales tax
5. Add $2.25 shipping for the first book; $.25 for each additional book

VISA or MasterCard are acceptable; be sure to include complete card number, expiration date, and your authorizing signature.
Prices effective January 1990, and subject to change without notice.

Send your order to: **Impact Publishers**

P.O. Box 1094, San Luis Obispo, CA 93406

[805] 543-5911